HOW TO BE GOOD AT ANYTHING

Neil Hingorani

Dedications

To Graham White White White –
Thanks for Glasto 2013 and 2014. Unbelievable gesture…
apologies for reversing over the tent.

To Jon – Thanks for making me write it.

British Library Cataloguing-in-Publication data
A catalogue record for this book is available from the British Library

ISBN: 978-1-7397623-0-8

Designed and typeset by Carnegie Scotforth Book Production

Cover Design by Cameron Holland

CONTENTS

Introduction

Now, before you say anything, I know what you're thinking. You're thinking Neil Hingorani... who's he? Well, it's fair to say that, unless you were a traffic cop in the West Midlands during the mid-1980s, you're unlikely to have heard of me. But who I am is not important, it's what I've got to tell you that's important.

Before we start, allow me to divulge some of my background. I am half Irish (Neil) and half Indian (Hingorani). As a member of the breed of half Irish half Indians, if you were to look at us on the spectrum of endangered species, we are one bar from the end marked extinct.

As a child my name stood out. Nobody in my school was called Neil (there were more Rumpelstiltskins than Neils) and nobody on earth was called Hingorani. But, I suppose I should be grateful; if it had turned out that my mum was Indian and my dad was Irish I would have been called Ranjeet McCarron. No disrespect to the Ranjeet McCarrons that walk this fine planet.

Now that the formalities are over it's down to business. I want you to read this book for one reason. I want to help you to be good at anything. That's right, anything! Before we start, let me just roll out a few gems to build that little bit of trust between us.

If you've ever struggled with maths, there's one simple piece of advice you need... *when you understand what the question is asking, the numbers take care of themselves.* Yes, maths is that simple. So, stop trying to fit the numbers together to get an answer that looks about right (which is what I used to do at school), spend your time on working out what the story is behind the question. That way, the numbers will fall into place.

Not convinced? Let's have a look at something else. Do It Yourself or as it's more commonly referred to, DIY. This was something that never topped my agenda until it dawned on me that I couldn't afford to pay a joiner to do my jobs around the house. There are two essential criteria which need to be satisfied for you to be good at DIY. First all you need to be skint and secondly you need patience. Slow down. Do the job slowly and you will find that, whereas before, you would probably have called someone in to do a job, nowadays you might just have a go yourself.

Am I winning you over yet? No? Yes? The non-believers amongst you want another example? Let's have a look at languages. You'll see students of all ages incinerating time by learning pages of vocabulary, much of it irrelevant. I can still remember the Latin word for tight rope walker, *funambulus* if you must know. I mean, the Romans are remembered for a number of notable achievements but, walking on a piece of rope between two buildings isn't one of them. The problem is new words rarely stick unless you actually speak the language on a daily basis, or bind them to something. Focusing on the verbs (doing words) allows other words to stick to them. All languages are built on verbs so don't pussyfoot around trying to remember obscure vocabulary that you might use once every four years. Verbs are the foundation of any language. End of.

You may not be surprised to learn that I didn't start life with the belief that you can be good at anything. It all started with a kid at school called Noddy White (he had Big Ears... Boom Boom). This lad was good at everything, and I mean everything. He'd never played chess before in his life and first game out he checkmated Mick Wile (scholarship maths) within about six moves.

One Monday when we got to school, there was a brand new table tennis table set up on the gym balcony. On the Friday, we went to play Grace Dieu Manor at a 'social evening' (that's what you do at private schools). It was a fairly good-natured event until Noddy destroyed their top three players at which point their headmaster hid Noddy's bat to bring the evening to a swift end.

This fellow Noddy White stuck in my mind as an anomaly (that word making its debut) to the people who say you can't be good at everything, because guess what... you actually *can*! That's right; you *can* actually be good at everything and it all starts with being good at anything... any *one* thing. That's different to saying that you can be *brilliant* at everything. That's not what I am saying or what this book is trying to do. But it can help you to be brilliant at something because, correct me if I am wrong, there have not been many people who've turned out brilliant at something without passing through good!

Anyway, where were we? If ever I heard someone say, "Well Neil, you can't be good at everything." I thought about this kid at school called Noddy White.

When I entered my teens, I became more aware of *how* people performed. I noticed that people who were very good at one thing, were often good at a number of other things. The opposite was *also* true. People who were last pick at football were often last pick at rugby and any other activity that might have been going on at school.

More importantly, I started to notice how people spoke. If ever I rang some of my friends to catch up, I could guarantee that, if I asked how they were, a major disaster had either just occurred or was looming on the horizon. Other friends, when asked the same question would respond with some upbeat message about how they were struggling to fit in 'S' Level Physics with First Eleven Football as well as dating the fittest girl in the school.

The common theme that emerged from people-watching in my youth, was that there seemed to be a link between how they spoke and how they performed. This whetted my appetite for further research. I knew I was onto something.

The ability to be good at anything started me on a mission which I have spent my life pursuing. Throughout my working life I have moved from job to job. Each time I learnt how to do a job, I left. At the time I didn't know why I felt the urge to leave each job once I had mastered it. I thought it was because I wanted to be rich but it wasn't... well it was a bit, but the real reason was that I was trying to uncover for me what was the ultimate *formula;* how to be good at anything. And I found it. Oh yes my friend, I found it.

Like all the best solutions in life, the formula for being good at anything is very simple. Building it, however, was slightly more of a challenge. In order to piece together the formula, I've worked in different parts of the world and worked on many different projects, learnt different languages and read over two hundred self-help books and probably the same number of biographies of famous people. I have qualified as a Chartered Surveyor, worked as a holiday rep, built houses, scrapped metal, lectured university students and worked in management consultancy. I have also written a dissertation on confidence as part fulfilment of my Masters in Education. However, this book has not been written from an academic perspective. It is based on my own experiences and watching those of other people.

This book is designed to take you on a journey to see for yourself how easy it is to be good at anything and for you to use my formula at your will. The chapters are filled with straightforward stuff but make no mistake, each one has had to work hard to earn its place in the book.

I decided to structure the book in four parts. The first three parts focus on the following items:

1. What are you *already* good at?

2. What do you *need to know* to be good at anything?

3. What do you *need to do* to be good at anything?

The book has been structured like this to show you how close you actually are to being good at anything. If you add what you're already good at in Part One to a few bits of information in Part Two, then you're two thirds of the way there. Part Three is just a list of things that you need to *do* to be good at anything and you might already be doing some of them anyway!

Part Four draws information from the first three parts and puts it into a simple story, which gives you the formula for being good at anything. It then teaches you how to perform confidently whatever it is you want to be good at, which to my mind should not be a *complete* waste of your time.

A lot of self-help books have been written with a focus on making money or they might have a religious slant. This book has neither. It is self-help for all, or those of you who prefer a label, let's call it self-help *lite*. I have tried to deliver advice in a light, sorry, *lite* hearted manner, but believe me when I say that each point is not to be taken *litely*. I have shown failures as well as successes because that's what happens in real life. It's also true that you learn a lot more from failures than you ever do from success and they're generally a bit more of a laugh.

Let's begin the journey...

PART ONE

WHAT ARE YOU ALREADY GOOD AT?

CHAPTER 1

Having a go

If you don't already think you're good at having a go at new stuff then how are you managing to read this sentence in the first place? You somehow persevered with reading long enough to be able to read. Forget about the perseverance bit for now because the first step in your reading was *you* having a go.

It's the same with that egg on toast you made this morning. You weren't born with an innate ability to make egg on toast, you learnt how to do it, after a few false starts, and again that started with you having a go. Think of every single thing you can do from tying your shoelaces to using a computer and they all started with you having a go. In fact, can you think of anything that you can do which *didn't start* with you having a go? My point exactly. So, we're agreed you're already an expert at having a go. This chapter is therefore just a bit of gentle revision for you.

Right then, so you've finally decided that you want to be good at something new, and I'm talking about anything, from swimming to biochemistry to being a comedian or simply being happy. The first thing you have to do is have a go and that means making a start.

Sounds simple enough doesn't it because it is simple?

It's just that you might have forgotten how simple it is. Actually, go to your first swimming lesson, your first basket weaving class, your first maths lecture, 'just do it' as a well-known brand which sounds like Mike also advises.

This is the first step. I'm told that the Aussies use an expression and it's 'have a go you mug'. I like that. You're not sitting there fretting about whether or not you are going to be a world beater, you're just having a go. And if it doesn't work out then who cares? You might look like a bit of an idiot but you're not going to die! Right then, before you read one more sentence in this book, you're going to get up and make that call or send that email or drive into town or whatever it is you need to do to get started. I'll be here to check up on you as soon as you get back. Go on then... off you go!

So, well done to you for making a start. It may be that your first class or lesson or experience of something turns out to be, how can I put it... less than satisfactory? Well that's just the way it goes. The challenge now is not giving up straightaway. I remember my first front crawl swimming lesson. Dreadful! It would have been easy to throw in the swimming towel on the first attempt, as I found myself slowly drowning over the course of an hour, but I just thought let's give it say five lessons and then if I still hate it, at least I gave it a go.

So it was week five and I was about ready to jack when something happened for the first time. I managed to breathe out under water. For a fish this is not such a big deal but for a human it's the starting point for real swimming. What this little achievement did was encourage me to carry on swimming. Now I never knew this when I was a kid, but as you get better at something a little change is triggered inside your head. This is called motivation. The ability to breathe out under water was motivation enough for me to sign up for another five lessons and then another ten and I still love my swimming today. But more about swimming later.

You see everybody's a bit nervous when they start something new. People tend to hide it well, so it doesn't make you some sort of freak because you're a bit nervous about something. It's normal... you freak!

As you know, not everything you have a go at will end in success. I occasionally think about those piano lessons when I was eight years old. I'm not sure what I hated more; the teacher, the lessons or my mum for making me go. There wasn't much in it. But do you know what? I wasn't interested in playing the piano back then and I'm not now. I had about ten lessons, okay maybe more like three, and didn't enjoy one of them, well, maybe the first one when she gave me pop and crisps. The thing is, I am not harking back thinking 'if only I'd had a go at it... I would have loved to play the piano' *because I did have a go* and it wasn't for me. Quite simply, I didn't enjoy it and so I didn't want to be good at it! And at the same time, I'm sure the world of piano is not mourning the loss.

One thing I *did* want to do was give up smoking. It must have taken me over 30 attempts because I stopped counting at 25, but I did it and in the last 25 years I have only had one cigarette (which was about three months ago strangely enough). To help me stop I bought a smoking diary and the single entry into the diary each day was 'Today I did not have a cigarette'. I used to look forward to bed time in order to write that one sentence each day but it was enough. Because each day I did not have a cigarette felt like a victory.

The difference between giving up smoking and learning to play the piano was the level of desire. If you do want to be good at something, you need to ask yourself one important question? Can I really be bothered? If the answer isn't a resounding 'Yes' then you might not want to waste your time starting... unless of course your boss has made you do it.

Here's another wee bit of advice... In order to give something a proper go you have to focus on it by making it a priority. When I was a self-employed builder, I knew how important it was to be able to use a computer, in terms of writing letters, preparing spreadsheets for accounts, sending emails but most importantly putting a bet on when the bookies were closed. Even though I was itching to get onto the building site in the morning to pick my first fight of the day with the brickie Pete Elliott, I didn't allow myself to go anywhere until I had spent one hour on the computer. By making it a priority, it turned itself into a habit and I reckon that good habits are just as hard to break as bad ones. I'd got myself into the good habit of using the computer and within one month, no more, I was computer literate.

The final paragraph is dedicated to those of you who ignored my advice from three pages ago and have still not made a start. You thought I'd forgotten about you, didn't you? Right then, not one more page of this book shall you read until you make a start... not one! So get on with it. Make a start! But if you don't, then don't be scared, nothing bad will happen I promise... except that maybe the monster that lives under your bed might get you.

Rani's Top Tip – Have a go you mug... what have you got to lose?

CHAPTER 2

Watching the experts

Years ago, when I was in the Lower Sixth at School, there was a period when only two people in our year were in the First XI football team, Noddy White and me. Noddy was in the team because he was the best player the school had ever had and I was in the team because I copied him. Okay, so true class shone through in the end and Noddy's stay in the First XI lasted three years, whereas I was dropped after five games. But the point is, I still managed to get into the team, and stay for a while, on the back of copying Noddy!

So, you see what can be achieved from simply watching other people in action. Just think about what you've picked up over the years from watching people do something well. If you think hard for a moment, you'll be able to trace back your negotiating skills to watching your Aunty Margaret return a perfectly good TV to CoCost after enjoying it for the last six months. Your kite flying skills can be traced back to watching your Uncle Geoff whose desire to be outside was generated by a lifetime listening to Aunty Maureen. You'll already have learnt numerous skills from watching other people. It's a fact. So, whatever it is you want to be good at... watch other people who are good at it and you will get better.

My mum's an osteopath and an acupuncturist in Burton on Trent. Last Christmas Eve she had a sore shoulder. Of course, there was no-one available to treat her because the staff had gone on holiday so she invited me to put a few acupuncture needles in her shoulder. She's the sort of person that if she asks you to do something then she likes you to get on with it. Think about it as more of an order than a request.

Not one to upset her, I used the electronic locator and put the needles into my mum's shoulder pretty well, even if I do say so myself. The thing is, I must have seen her do it a thousand times on patients in the past and so when it came to me putting the needles in, it felt like I already knew what to do. Even if I did forget to take one of them out when I'd finished.

So hopefully you're getting the idea that there's a lot of information that can be gleaned simply by watching someone, even if you have absolutely no experience of doing that job yourself. By watching people your whole life it can make *you* subconsciously just as capable of doing what they're doing.

When I was working as a surveyor for the Children's Society, I had a site meeting with this guy who was giving me some advice about building work on a property that the society owned. We got chatting and he mentioned the fact that he'd built a house. I said in passing that I used to refurbish property and built a few houses myself and what an excellent learning experience it was to manage tradesmen. So, he said to me, "I didn't use tradesmen I just built it myself".

I replied, "Oh bollocks, did you build it yourself."

So he said, "Do you want to see the photos?"

I said, just to humour him, "Go on then, show me the photos".

He starts off with "Right, this is me driving the JCB and digging out the footings. That's me and my brother putting the damp proof membrane in. That's me putting the second lift up on the scaffolding after we'd laid the bricks and blocks on ground floor level... there's another one of me doing the first fix electrics". And in fairness to him the final picture showed a cracking house. So, I said to him, well I suppose if you're a builder then, sooner or later you can pick up each of the trades. To which he replied, "I'm not a builder, I'm an estate agent!" Boom Boom.

It turns out that when he was a kid, he'd watched his dad build a house from start to finish and just thought it was a normal thing to do. You know... build an entire house by yourself.

Now here's the interesting bit, because the 'watch and learn' theory not only works with people who are good at their job but also with people who are crap. Going back to when I was a kid at school there were some pretty poor teachers and it amazed me how they'd ever got the job. 'O' Level Biology stands out as a school low light.

The teacher's name was Mr Hunt. Fate had somehow conspired to mis-spell his surname by a single letter. This bloke couldn't stand me, and in fairness it didn't take long before the feeling was reciprocated. I think Mr Hunt resented the fact that my dad wanted me to become a doctor, which is a bit harsh when you consider that every single Indian father since 1929 has wanted his son to become a doctor.

There was another minor obstacle hindering a career in medicine; I hated biology. This probably had something to do with how I was taught and who was teaching me because Mr Hunt's real talent in life was to make a straightforward subject appear highly complex.

In my life I do a fair amount of lecturing and what helped me more than anything was reflecting on how Mr Hunt and other bad teachers taught me. I remember thinking, "If I just do the opposite of how I was taught at school, then I should be okay." So I made a list:

1. Bad teachers made lessons at school boring – Do the opposite and make them interesting.

2. Bad teachers made the subject complicated – Do the opposite and make it simple.

3. Bad teachers had teacher's pets – Do the opposite and don't have favourites.

4. Bad teachers didn't like me – Do the opposite and try to like all the students.

5. Bad teachers held a grudge for life if you did something wrong – Do the opposite by punishing promptly and forgiving soon after.

6. Bad teachers took themselves very seriously – Do the opposite and be prepared to laugh at yourself now and then.

These are the invaluable lessons I learnt about teaching from watching bad teachers in action. I probably learnt more from one bad teacher than all the good ones combined. How crazy is that? We're all conditioned to believe that we must learn from the experts and nobody else. Of course, we can learn from the experts. But learning from the idiots... now that's a skill.

Rani's Top Tip – If you can learn from the experts *and* the idiots then you can learn from anybody.

CHAPTER 3

Using trial and error

This is one of my favourite pieces of advice. How many times do you hear about the need for having a plan? Whether it's a lesson plan prepared by a teacher, a flight plan drafted by a pilot, building plans drawn up by an architect or an escape plan drawn up by an inmate in a high security prison; they all do the same job, which is give you a strategy for achieving something. Now there's absolutely nothing wrong with that and I'm definitely one for planning, especially before a negotiation where there's a bit of money at stake. At the same time, in life you will very often be faced with a situation where you haven't prepared a plan. What do you do then?

Think back to when you were a child. There was no planning then, was there? If you wanted to climb a tree you just had a go, didn't you? You climbed up a bit, fell off, got up, climbed a bit further this time, fell off and got up again. And eventually you climbed the tree. The same thing is true when you first rode a bike.

Let's go back in time even further, to when you were an infant. I've never seen one writing out a strategy for being able to stand up and get to the other side of the room. I didn't bear witness to one infant on the internet for two hours downloading 15 different methods of learning how to walk. So how did these amazing children finally learn to stand up, walk and then run for that matter?

Good old trial and error. That's how they did it! There were no meetings with 11 babies sitting around a boardroom table taking turns to elaborate on the best of way of walking. Can you imagine what that would be like?

> The meeting starts off with the chair baby. "On the agenda today babies, is walking. Now I know that a number of you have been struggling with this particular concept for over three months now, so it's probably time for us to obtain feedback on our individual experiences so that we can create a proper strategy for this concept of what was it called again… ah yes, walking".

> "Joshua, would you like to begin?"

> "Thank you, Michael. On a personal note, a certain amount of progress has been made in what I prefer to call vertical movement, however using only two foot or feet, I think that's the correct term, to balance on, I am unfortunately not experiencing a great deal of success." … and it goes on.

On the occasions I watched my daughter learning to walk, I never got the impression that there was a plan in place and it never seemed to matter. The procedure seemed very straightforward. Nancy attempted walking then fell, got up, had another go then fell again. But what nobody could see, was that inside her head, she was learning from each setback. Her mind was not clouded by the energy sapping emotion of failure because she didn't understand failure. Failure to an infant does not exist. It's just feedback, positive and negative. In her head she was saying "This seems to work, that's not very helpful, next time I am going to try..."

But the best thing about trial and error is that *you* are already an expert. You have used this technique successfully for years and you know it works, so why bury it at the bottom of your wardrobe between your 3-D specs and your Donald Duck tracksuit, dismissing it as something that only a child would use? It's for adults too!

Some years ago, I had a high-profile position (for me) with a large construction company which sounds like Marillion. Sadly the company is no more (... that's what you get for operating a zero alcohol policy at dinner time). I was earning good money, the best day rate I had ever been on equating to £400 per day which works out at about £100,000 per year give or take. My contract ended on Christmas Eve of that same year and I was confident that I would soon find work as I had never been unemployed for more than a few weeks at a time. Little did I know the scale of the recession of 2008... God bless the banking crisis!

I started brightly in January 2009, looking for new surveying contracts at around the same money. Pretty soon I realised that the contracting market had fallen off a cliff and that I would have to apply for a permanent position. No problem, it just meant that instead of looking for jobs that paid £100,000 per annum, it meant looking for jobs paying around £50,000.

February came and a large dose of realism began to

kick in. I was now applying for surveying jobs at £35,000 per annum. These were again proving very difficult to secure so I went for an interview as an estate agent. We were now in the paying arena of around £20–25,000 per annum and working on Saturdays. I still wasn't quite over the fact that I'd had to go to *school* on Saturdays, never mind work on a Saturday. Do they know who I am?

So, it's the end of March and I'm not even working as an estate agent. April saw my ego undergo further trauma as I applied for a job as a business space manager with Regus in Cannock on a salary of £10,000 per annum. (It could be worse couldn't it…?) I was then told that this life-changing salary, in a bad way, had been withdrawn and the post would now be offered on a commission only basis (… maybe not).

It was May 2009, the beginning of summer to many, but to me, the official end of my career. I was at rock bottom, or so I thought. It turned out that rock bottom was still some way down but at least I was heading in the right direction. *Strangely enough it was this particular experience that gave me the idea for the book.*

Time passed and money disappeared from my account with the speed of a Catholic leaving church when mass is over. It was June 2009 and I was now applying for jobs as a door-to-door salesman, commission only I'll have you know, and still receiving a steady stream of rejections. By that stage, I think if I'd applied for a job as a motorway traffic cone I would have been rejected. This was the rock bottom which I had struggled so hard to reach. My surveying career was now just a hazy dream recollected with fondness along with England winning the World Cup and the old one-pound note.

And then it happened. I got a job... well, a sort of job in that I got paid for doing something. My brother-in-law needed somebody to drive a van to pick up and drop off gear for him while he gave presentations around the country. It paid for bits and bobs and got me out of the house. Before I knew it, he'd offered me some part-time consulting work and then from that I secured a full-time job as a lecturer at a local University on £44,500 per annum.

So, by using trial and error I had travelled from slick senior surveyor to virtuous van driver to likeable lecturer all in the space of five months and 13 days. Arguably the process of getting a job was similar to a baby learning to walk but the difference was that, whereas *I* was frightened of failure, the baby wasn't. Some fears were real, such as running out of money, and some were perceived... what will other people think about me? But all of these fears took energy from me which I needed to put into actually getting a job. Trial and error is simple, the difficult bit is taking the learning from each experience whilst leaving the emotion behind.

Rani's Top Tip – Never dismiss trial and error. Sometimes it's all you've got.

CHAPTER 4

Trusting your instincts

Running my own business some years ago, I decided to move the set-up from my house to an office shared with my parents. We had two photocopiers. The one I had been using had consistently delivered good results and the one my dad was using wasn't great but it did have a service agreement which meant that all major repairs were covered by paying a small monthly fee.

We didn't need two copiers between us so I asked my dad which one we should get rid of. Well, I was only 35 at the time, how could I possibly trust myself to make a decision of such magnitude? The upshot was that he said we should get rid of mine. No reason given... or none worth remembering.

I knew it was a mistake but whereas my dad was a successful surgeon and I was more of a... how can I put it... serial trouble maker, I ran with his decision. You can of course guess what happened. I don't need to finish the story but I will. One week (one week!) after selling my photocopier, my old man's copier packed up completely which somehow voided the service agreement. We were then buying a third one for a comforting *seven times* the sale price of mine. If I had only trusted my own instincts, which were screaming at me, and guided my dad, this situation would have been avoided. He was a reasonable guy after all. But I didn't.

It's a big thing learning to trust yourself. Everyone has instincts which help them make decisions but for some reason we don't always listen to them. I have learnt, over the years, that when my heart rate speeds up, coupled with losing my appetite, then I am going against my instincts. As soon as I rectify the situation my body goes back to normal.

Try to work out how *your* body responds to *you* when you are doing something it's not happy with. I promise there'll be some message it's sending you. Learn to listen to yourself. You can do this through a quiet walk, a bit of relaxation, or a full specification meditation. All these things work by allowing your mind to settle down, enabling solutions to rise to the surface.

Imagine, a good friend of yours asks you to go into business with her. She's great fun and you love the business idea but, unfortunately, her track record shows three bankruptcies, a corporate administration and two receiverships, not to mention an investigation by the Serious Fraud Office. I know it's a difficult one but what do your instincts tell you to do?

Here's another one; you're heading for the train station one night and you have a choice of walking down two streets. The first street will take you two minutes to reach the station but it's narrow and dimly lit and there are three big lads, wearing hoodies and balaclavas, trying to break through a door using a crowbar. The second street will take you five minutes to get there. However, it's well lit, there are plenty of passers-by, and your favourite shop, *Sausage Rolls and Pasties*, is sitting in the middle of the street with that cracking smell of baking pastry heading straight for your nostrils. Which street should you take?

We use and trust our instincts all the time, but a lot of the time we're not aware that we're actually doing this. Ask yourself, how do I feel about going into business with a financial car crash? You will get the right answer. Ask yourself is it worth saving three minutes' walk but risking your life to achieve it and again you will get the right answer. Just as you always have done.

Now, I'm going to tell you a story about a time when I did trust my instincts. My parents and I were involved in some property deals together, where I was to use the NEW shared photocopier which was so painfully acquired. Some of these deals involved buying land in Spain. I remember one time we were trying to buy some land in a small fishing town called Garrucha. The problem was we were trying to buy this site before we had sold another one.

I'll give you some idea of the numbers but most of the files have been chucked so I can't remember exactly the costs involved. The cost of the site was approximately 700,000 euros and we'd put a deposit down of 175,000 euros. Now, unlike in England whereby you have to complete a transaction within a definite timescale, in Spain there is more flexibility. This meant that we kept delaying completion, spinning the purchase out until,

18 months after exchange of contracts, we were press ganged into paying the balance; 525,000 euros to be exact. There was only one small problem. We didn't have it.

Somehow, I managed to cobble the money together by sinking to depths in my behaviour I never knew existed as I extracted money from friends, family, the bank and anyone who had the misfortune to bump into me immediately prior to completion.

When the time came to make the last payment, I travelled to Spain feeling the need to undertake some final checks on the land to see if it was still worth the price we were paying for it. In order to do this, I met with, amongst others, local estate agent Gerardo who I'd done a couple of deals with previously.

Gerardo went through details of other recent sales in the area with me and as we sat in a café in Garrucha, it slowly dawned on me that the land was worth about half of what we were paying for it. I'm sorry Gerardo. Could you just run that by me again? It's worth *half* of what we're paying for it?

This meant we couldn't possibly buy the land after all. But, we'd still lose the deposit and were now certified financially dead. The end is here in the port of Garrucha on a dull Friday lunchtime amongst the cold chips, a half empty bottle of San Miguel and an ash tray where a Marlboro Light had been stubbed out; my business was over.

THE END.

But wait, there was hope. Gerardo suddenly remembered something he'd forgotten. His evidence was wrong? It was all a big mistake we were going to be saved after all.

"Neil" exclaimed Gerardo, "where you live in England?"

"Lichfield" I said, losing a fraction of confidence regarding this potential solution.

"Can you tell me if there is Aston Martin garage where to buy DB7 Vantage?"

To this day I will never forget that question. Read it again. I mean... the word 'insensitive' springs to mind. I have to give myself a bit of credit here because I did see the funny side of it. His business was booming while my business was bombing. Bloody Perfect.

The thing was, when I woke up the next day (or was it the day after?), I felt at peace. I was happy. I was happy because I had made the right decision to heap 175,000 euros into a pile, put a match to it and walk away from the deal. I told my parents what I had decided. They weren't happy but they accepted the decision even if my mum couldn't resist a monthly reminder for the next seven years. The worst had happened and I felt great. A year later it turned out the land was worth less than 50,000 euros. Now that's what I call a property crash. My instincts had served me well and I had learnt from Photocopiergate.

Before you feel too sorry for me, this story does have a happy ending. Exactly one year later, we sold a parcel of land for a whopping ten times the amount we paid for it. If we hadn't dumped the Garrucha land we'd never have felt strong enough in our negotiating position to ask for such a price on this second parcel.

We all have instincts and most of the time we trust them. The important thing is to recognise when we're going against them and how our body responds when we're doing this. Look out for the warning signals that flash from your onboard computer and respond appropriately. You'll know you're on the right track when the warning signals disappear. You have the technology. I promise you. Everyone has.

Rani's Top Tip – Learn to trust your instincts... they're a great tool for making good decisions.

CHAPTER 5

Making notes

I know what you're thinking... make notes? How come, when I'm already good at making notes? Well, just allow me to come back to you on that in a minute, but first let me tell you what used to happen at Birmingham University Dental School in the bit before I got expelled.

The lecturer used to speak at 214 miles per hour and if you didn't get it down, the chances were that *he* couldn't remember what he'd said if you asked him to repeat something. You were constantly asking your neighbour about the bits you'd missed. "Listen mate, what did Alien Head just say? He was going that fast..."

"Don't ask me mate, I haven't got a clue I'm still on the date." ...or something like that.

The only way to get round it was putting our mate Daz in the middle of the table; three of us sat on either side of him in arrowhead formation as the notes filtered their way down to both ends of the table. This system also worked well in exams... for the people who passed of course!

Nowadays, the ability to write notes while somebody speaks is not quite as important. There's so much material that you can obtain for yourself from the internet that you don't even need the speaker to give you the information. All you have to do is print out what you need in advance, jot a few personal notes on the side: <u>underline</u> this, I don't understand that, this sounds important... you get the idea? (Notice how I have cleverly underlined the word underline).

So why is it still so important to take notes when you're studying something or listening to someone? Because, by writing it in your own words, it means that your brain has processed the information. This means that the information stays with you, which is fairly useful if you're trying to be good at something.

Even if you're just taking down what the speaker has said verbatim (another first), you probably wrote it down because you got the feeling it was important and even though you didn't totally understand it, you could spend a few minutes that evening examining what you wrote down and do some further research.

It can't be a completely crazy idea. People have been taking notes as some sort of memory aid since the days when the house-pet doubled up as the evening meal. Anyway, while we're on the subject of food, if you were to walk into a restaurant back then and order say velociraptor on toast, chances are the waitress would be scratching your order onto a sandstone slab using the beak of a dead toucan.

The thing I notice most whenever I'm giving a lecture is that often students will bring an iPhone, an iPod or an iPad but what they really need is an iPen; a pen which could give you on the spot advice such "Hingo, if you don't pick me up and drag me across the page in the next five seconds... I will properly sort you out". If you think that sounds ridiculous, last Tuesday my mate Andy from Share club, paid for a round of drinks with his watch.

To take notes, all you need is a notebook and of course a pen. The book need be nothing special, just any old book that you can write in, but each time you make an entry you must remember to put the date by it. The date is important because it allows you to put your notes in the right order. When the information is positioned in a logical order it makes your notes easy to understand.

Oh, I can hear you whining now, "But you said I'm already good at taking notes, so why's that?" Well think about the notes you'll have written in the past. They'll probably fall into one of these two categories:

1. Something you have understood.

2. Something you may not have understood but sounded important so you've written it down to investigate later.

So my answer to you is, if that's all there is to note-taking how can you *not* be good at it? The thing is, it doesn't matter how bad your notes are, because it's not the quality of the notes that are important, it's the fact that you've made some notes that's important. This is because your notes act as a story of the event and when you come to re-read those notes with all the scrawl and drawings and bits and bobs, it will bring back to you what you heard on the day along with other items that you thought you'd forgotten. Even a little drawing of the lecturer's beer belly will remind you of who gave the lecture and what was said.

Remember you don't have to be an Olympic champion at taking notes, just the act of making notes will reinforce whatever it is you are trying to learn. Now that wasn't too painful, was it?

Rani's Top Tip – Any notes are good notes.

PART TWO

WHAT DO YOU NEED TO KNOW TO BE GOOD AT ANYTHING?

CHAPTER 6

Understand what's happening when things go wrong

This chapter is about how we interpret events when things have gone wrong in our quest to be good at something. When I was growing up and something went wrong, I felt that there were two external forces acting against me:

1. Luck
2. God

The feedback I was getting from failures were put into these two boxes. Right then let's first consider luck. As a child, I always believed I was unlucky. I can't remember any defining moment that sparked this belief, it was just a general belief that existed on my hard drive along with other beliefs such as I am very good at French, good at football and not very good at all at biology.

In order to counter this belief, I became very superstitious. Superstition is something we use when we're concerned that our forces of luck need a bit of help. Think about it like an insurance policy we take out just in case Lady Luck is having a day off. Let me give you an example of how the 'policy' works; I need to be on time for my meeting in Madrid on Wednesday morning, I do hope the plane isn't late. I know, I'll eat a piece of carrot cake when I get to the airport. This is because, once, many years ago, when I expected a flight to be delayed, I ate a piece of dried-up carrot cake at the airport café and the plane left on time.

Fortunately, my beliefs about luck changed when one day my wife bought me a book about luck. The only thing I can remember about this book was that it gave a solid argument for the difference between lucky people and unlucky people. The essence of it was that "lucky people *believe* they are lucky and unlucky people *believe* they are unlucky". When I say solid argument, it might just have been the previous sentence I remember. Anyway, after reading that book, I made a decision to change how I thought about luck.

Changing my *belief* about being lucky was like flicking a switch. Now that I believed I was lucky, I started to notice occasions where I was lucky and this magnified my feeling of luck. At the same time, I began to overlook moments where I received bad luck which, in turn, minimised the emotion of feeling unlucky.

The combined effect of these two changes in my behaviour made me believe I was even luckier. Now that I truly believed I was lucky, I was able to eliminate the superstitious behaviours which I had clung onto for all those years. It was over for the carrot cake. Never again would I be held to ransom by that third-rate airport snack.

I can appreciate that the change from believing you are unlucky to believing you are lucky may be too big a leap for some. To help you do it, another way to think about luck is to consider it as something which drops in to help you when the hard work has been done. It's a bit like making a carrot cake, putting it in the oven then falling asleep and waking up two hours later to find that someone has taken it out of the oven for you.

My mate Paddy believes that, "luck is preparation meeting opportunity," which is another saying which links luck with work and I believe this is also true. It basically means that once you've done the hard work (preparation) then, when the time comes, luck will appear like a visit from your generous Aunty Mandy whom you've not seen for a while.

To reinforce this, have a look at the following scenarios:

Let's say you have a history exam coming up and there are five topics with one question on each topic. You have to answer say three questions out of five. Now consider:

1. If you had revised all five topics and got an A then this is not luck. You had done the work and deserved a good grade. If one or even two questions had been difficult to answer, then you would still have been able to fall back on three solid questions.

2. If you had revised for three topics and got an A then that would be lucky. This is because if one question out of the three had been difficult to answer, you would not have had a fall-back position and would have had to answer it. You were therefore lucky that you could answer all three questions fully.

3. If, however, you had only revised for one topic and got an F then that would not be unlucky. This is because the highest mark you could have got is 33% which is an E. An F (less than 30%) would not therefore be unlucky in this instance, it would be entirely deserved.

You see there is a difference between being unlucky and being lazy and I guess this was the point that Paddy was trying to make. Let me give you some advice, don't confuse bad luck with lack of preparation.

Okay, now let's move on to God. Now before you start rolling your eyes and thinking, I thought Hingo said this book had nothing to do with religion, I want to reassure you that I will not be delivering a single religious message within these pages. That would be a bit rich seeing as I haven't been inside a church for more than a decade. However, it's a bit difficult to write a chapter about external forces without giving God a mention.

By the way, feel free to substitute the word God for Jehovah, Life, Allah, The Universe, The Subconscious Mind, The Force or whatever you like. I'm going to use the word God as it's the term I understand... as far as I'm able to understand an eternal, dimensionless and all powerful being.

Cast your mind back to the day Roger Federer was playing Andy Murray in the Wimbledon Tennis Final of 2012. The backdrop to this game was that Roger Federer was sitting on 12 Grand Slam titles, while poor Andy was busting his gut to get a first. Even Federer's Mrs wouldn't have minded old Roger letting this one go.

Anyway, Roger is serving for the match and our heart is breaking for Andy who is about to lose four grand slam finals on the trot. We are all thinking "surely God wants Andy to win"... well God was probably sitting up in heaven with a Pimms enjoying the game not knowing who was going to win.

The singular best piece of wisdom I ever received on the whole God subject was this (which I have stolen from Andrew Master's classic book called Being Happy): God has no favourites.

As it turned out, Andy did lose the match but exactly four weeks after that Wimbledon Final he went on to win the Olympic Tennis Final for Great Britain in that very same stadium and guess who his opponent was... none other than Mr Roger Federer! This win was the catalyst for Andy who, six weeks later, went on to win his first grand slam final at the US open in 2012. A year later, he was back at Wimbledon where he beat Novak Djokovic in the Final to become the first British player to win Wimbledon since Fred Perry in 1936... what a guy!

You see, God has no favourites... not even Roger Federer who, may I remind you, as well as becoming the most successful tennis player of all time (for a bit), was also a loser in *eleven* grand slam finals himself.

Rani's Top Tips:
1. Luck is believing you are lucky.
2. Luck is something you get when the hard work has been done.
3. God (Life, The Force etc.) has no favourites.

CHAPTER 7

As you start to improve your motivation increases

When I was at school, I had to study A Level Chemistry. It was probably my worst subject because I had even less interest in Chemistry than I did in Mr Hunt's Biology lessons which is going some. So it came as a bit of a shock to me when I went to university and I had to study a subject called Biochemistry. This performed the not inconsiderable job of combining the blinding boredom of biology with the cranial conundrums of chemistry. My notetaking deteriorated like a radioactivity decay curve so that by week six, just an occasional word could be found trespassing on each clean page of my notebook.

But much as I tried to avoid thinking about the inevitable, the examination was looming at the end of the year and I needed to pass to stay on the course.

So, I started picking away at the subject very slowly at first and, believe me, it was slow and painful but through some blinkered act of perseverance I managed to make small inroads. The strange thing was, the more I understood about biochemistry, the more I enjoyed it. As a result, the more motivated I became to learn. If

I was to break it down for you, the steps looked a bit like this:

1. I persevered enough to understand the basics

2. Understanding the basics increased my interest

3. The increased interest motivated me to learn

4. The more I learnt the more I became interested

This experience taught me a very important lesson; once you reach a critical mass of understanding, *anything* can become interesting... even biochemistry. You'll see that steps three and four create a self-perpetuating cycle of learning.

I'm shaking my head while I write this because I still can't believe it's true. A subject in which initially I had absolutely zero interest, turned out to be my favourite subject. Now the fact that I got expelled from university a year later for a totally different reason is neither here nor there, because when it came to biochemistry, I'd got it sussed.

Rani's Top Tip – The more you learn ... the more motivated you become to learn.

CHAPTER 8

You are responsible for your own improvement

Right then, it's time to give you some news which might come as a real shock. If you want to be good at something, nobody else can do it for you. You are responsible for your own improvement.

So, and I'm spelling it out to you now, if you're not getting better, it's your fault. Oh yes, it is, amigo. When you accept the fact that *you* are in charge of improving yourself, then you have taken responsibility.

Have you ever watched a Premier League football manager being interviewed after he's lost a game? You have? Excellent. How many times have you heard the manager express, in some way, his disappointment with the referee's performance? I now find myself waiting for them to mention the referee. The manager conveniently forgets that his star striker has missed three sitters whilst his centre back was sent off for a two-footed tackle. To him, defeat was caused solely by the referee, whose single mistake in the entire afternoon was his inability to detect that a member of the opposing team had dived in order to win a penalty, which was subsequently scored.

It makes you want to be a referee, doesn't it? In five years' time, when Premier League matches are being refereed by the local policeman... you'll know the reason why. You'll also know the moment when *you* have started to take responsibility for your own mistakes because that's when you'll stop hearing yourself blame other people for your lack of progress.

If you've had a go at sorting a problem and I mean a real go and it hasn't worked, then fair enough. You can moan and whinge for a bit but after that get back to work. But blaming the referee, or anyone else for that matter, is such a cop out. Try a different tack, my old fruit, and remember that each failure takes you one step closer to success.

One of my friends at work is called Mary and she suffers from migraines. Every time she had a migraine I would say, "Mary, why don't you go and see my mum. She's an acupuncturist and she'll get rid of those migraines for you."

"Well, how do you know it's going to work Neil?"

"I don't Mary, it's just that the previous 273 migraine patients have been cured so I'd say there's a reasonable chance your treatment would prove successful."

"But Burton's a long way from Wolverhampton Neil and how much does she charge?"

"Look, I'll drive you there and I'll pay for it myself," I'd say to her but still she wouldn't go.

To this day Mary is still suffering from migraines. Unbelievable. It's difficult to be sympathetic with someone if each time they're offered a solution it's rejected out of hand.

You have to ask yourself if you are one of these people who like to get attention because they're having a hard time. I call them "Poor me". Maybe *you* prefer the attention you get from people feeling sorry for you than the feeling you get from succeeding or in this case getting better. If this is the case then you need to cop on to yourself and change your ways... pronto!

Right then let's go back to swimming for a moment. Do you remember me telling you that it took me five weeks to learn to breathe out under the water? You probably got the impression that I'd got front crawl sussed after that. Well, that's not exactly the whole story. You see I started learning to swim in November 2011 but by March 2017 I still couldn't swim front crawl for more than one and a half lengths of the pool. Now that's what I call progress! There I was, after six years of sustained effort, splashing and spluttering my way up the pool and then halfway down it. With 2cc of oxygen in my lungs remaining, I was forced to walk the last ten metres to the end of the pool in full view of the *Baywatch*esque female lifeguard. At which point I would have *another* go at completing two full lengths of the 25-metre pool.

During that six-year crusade I tried swimming club in the local gym, I tried following Swim Smooth on the internet, my brother-in-law Paddy gave me advice, I tried another swimming club in Tamworth then I went back to my old swimming club in Lichfield but nothing worked. I tried everything to break the two-length barrier, but my sinking legs formed a perfect anchor which my poor old body worked frantically to raise from the swimming pool floor.

So, realising my own limitations and as a sort of last resort (because I could never actually give up) I spoke to the swimming coach, Ben, who had found himself compelled to give me some free advice due to the distress this sight was causing him. Four half-hour lessons later and I could swim ten lengths of the pool non-stop. Stands back in amazement.

My point is that it was nobody else's fault that I couldn't swim properly. I couldn't ring up one of those accident help lines on TV and claim 15 grand because I couldn't swim properly. It was my problem that I couldn't swim properly. Nobody else had caused that problem and nobody else could fix it for me. But, by taking responsibility for my lack of progress, it meant that each time I choked on water, it allowed me to learn from it. That meant I was always improving, even if it did take me six years to swim two lengths of front crawl.

You might already have picked up that the lesson in this chapter is not just about responsibility, it's also about perseverance. But now that we've touched on the subject of getting a coach, it's nearly time for the next chapter.

Rani's Top Tip – If you don't take responsibility for your own mistakes then how do you expect to learn from them? It will always be somebody else's fault.

CHAPTER 9

If you need a coach get one

Okay, by now you've had a real go at improving under your own steam; you've taken notes, talked to people, looked on the internet, seen a podcast or a lecture and you're still not getting better. It's time, my friend, to get a coach.

This applies to absolutely anything; if you want to be happy then get a counsellor (life coach), if you want to improve your ability to manage your finances, get an accountant (money coach) and if you want to be good at swimming then get a swimming coach (coach-coach). But how do you choose a coach? Read on.

When I was a kid and doing my 'O' Levels (now called GCSEs), I remember checking my grades and this very interesting relationship appeared. It was basically that the more I liked the teacher, the better the grade I got. Think about it for a second because that's quite an important statement. You see the reason I liked the teacher was simply because he liked me.

Let me give you an example. Along with the majority of subjects I studied at school, I had minimal interest in French. My only incentive to learn French would have been the chance to talk to a few French girls but I knew there wouldn't have been much chance of that in our favourite holiday outpost on the West Coast of Ireland. So, what chance did I have of getting a top grade in French? It's not looking great, is it? There was a French teacher at school called Johnnie Walker (honestly). Well, it just turned out that Johnnie Walker loved the idea of me missing his lessons to do something far more important, like spending the morning travelling to Lancashire to play Manchester Grammar at football. As a weird sort of thank you to Johnnie, I gave French everything and ended up with an 'A' in my 'O' level. You can guess what I got in Biology, can't you.

This link, between grade achieved and the relationship with the teacher (coach), operated in every single subject in school and continued on through higher education.

So hopefully you can now see that there is one essential requirement your coach needs to satisfy. Your coach has to like you. How many times have you heard that? My bet is never. This only properly dawned on me whilst I was writing this book.

I went on a diving course a couple of years ago and the instructor didn't take to me at all. That's not a problem. I don't expect everyone to like me, but the problem it created was that during the sessions I was a nervous wreck. I couldn't hear his instructions because I was so anxious. As a result, I came away with a fear of diving and a negative belief about my own diving capabilities which were already pretty crap before I started the course. Do I think the opposite would have happened if the coach had liked me? Quite simply, yes. I never got into diving, and after my experience it's not really such a surprise, is it?

The second key role of a coach is to reinforce the basics. The reason for this is that once you understand the basic principles you can build on them. And guess who told me this? You've got it, the great Noddy White who operated with the wisdom of the Dalai Lama at the age of 17. If you don't get a grasp of the basic principles of what you're doing its very difficult for any new information to stick. As a coach, it's so important to teach the basics and as a student your job is to master them.

But what if you get the wrong coach? An important lesson I've learned from my 37 jobs since I've left school was that... wait for it... get the drums rolling... you can't change people. Simple. You can't change people. You can, coax, cajole, reason, shout, get mardy, you can even threaten to grass someone up to their mum but you cannot change people. What I mean by this is you can't make someone do something they don't want to do. So why is this relevant to me I hear you ask. Well, my good friend, the simple answer is that if someone is coaching you in a way that is not helping you improve, then it's unlikely they will change their method of coaching to help you.

I have a very simple rule of thumb which I use to help me work out whether a coach, or anybody else for that matter, is the right person; if someone is doing a job for me and I'm worried about the job they're doing then I've got the wrong person and I need to get rid. Pronto!

If someone is doing a job for me and I'm *not* worried about the job they are doing, then I know I've got the right person and I need to keep them. This is because the right person will be doing the worrying for me.

The messages I need to give you with regard to a coach are:

1. If you need a coach, get one.

2. The coach needs to like you.

3. A good coach will focus on reinforcing the basics.

4. If you're worried the coach isn't helping you improve then you're probably right and you need to get rid.

Rani's Top Tip – If you need a coach, get one but take your time to get the right person.

CHAPTER 10

Never underestimate your environment

I'm sitting here in front of my computer holding two items. In my left hand is a class prize for academic achievement at my primary school. It's a book called *Living Free* by Joy Adamson with a brief inscription in it, along with the year the prize was awarded (1975). Wildlife is not my thing and I've never read a word of it but that's not the point as you'll see. In my right hand I am holding a class list for 1979. It shows me sitting firmly at the bottom of the class by 24 marks.

Four short years between these two events, so what do you think happened? Don't cheat but try and answer before you look at the paragraph below.

Most likely you've guessed at an illness of some kind which kept me away from school, or more likely that my parents divorced, or somebody close to me died. The answer is none of the above. I simply changed schools.

That was it. I moved from a primary school where I was very happy to a private school where I was very unhappy. You could almost date my academic landslide to the day I went to this new school. And this deterioration continued as I went to the next expensive private school. You see *I* hadn't changed but the environment around me had and what a difference it made to my performance.

When I say environment, what I'm really talking about is the people around you and not the place you're working. I'm a great believer that you can be depressed at the perfect address and ready for fun in the world's biggest slum because it's the people that create your environment.

I'm sure you can relate to this. Have you ever sat next to somebody at work who doesn't like you? You can feel the energy drain out of your body. Now what happens the next day when you've been told to switch desks and now you're sitting next to one of your best mates. It's like you're working for a different company. The work becomes effortless. It's easy to sit next to somebody great and work hard. This is the effect that a simple change in your environment has on you.

Some years ago, I worked for a company called Antler Homes as a land buyer. I can remember how long I lasted... six weeks and four days. I started on a Monday got fired on a Friday and there was a bank holiday somewhere in between. It was such a short duration that I can't even remember the twat's name who fired me. I can however remember the reason. The boss said it was because my technical knowledge was weak. When I questioned him further, he said it was because I didn't know what the term 'attenuation' meant (as reasons for firing someone go, I'd heard better). If you're interested to know, it means 'drain' which is pretty much what I could see my career going down after that meeting.

I can remember the morning clearly. I arrived at work at 8.30am, got fired at 9.30am, cleared my desk by 10am and by 10.45 I was in the Little Chef at Branston Turn with an Olympic Breakfast in front of me. The real reason I got fired was because the boss thought I was a snob as some wise guy (possibly me) told him I'd been to a private school. The irony was that I was probably one of 0.5% of public schoolboys who left *without* a designer accent.

Not long after, I started a job working for a company which sounds like Marillion, where I worked for a top bloke called Patrick (Paddy6 in *The Perfect Match*). This bloke liked me and trusted me to get on with the job. As a result, I turned into the Deal Dog. Every deal I touched, I completed. It became a bit of a joke in the office. Everything I touched at Marillion turned to gold and everything I touched at Antler turned to shit.

So, what had suddenly changed? I had not gone from being a crap surveyor to a brilliant surveyor. I was probably quite good at the job. But I had gone from an environment where I was isolated to one where I was supported. I hadn't changed, but the environment had.

So, whatever it is that you're trying to be good at, make sure your environment is right. It really does make a difference to your performance... just ask Fernando Torres. Okay you say to me, if you're so clever, how do I know if I am in the wrong environment? Easy. You're not having fun.

Rani's Top Tip – If you're not enjoying yourself, then you're in the wrong place.

CHAPTER 11

How to practise

One of my favourite sayings as a lecturer is 'don't confuse effort with results'. Hard work on its own is no good if you wish to improve because it's about working *smart* not *hard*. Why is that? Because if you're not working smart then you're wasting valuable time and time is the most precious commodity you have. You see, my friend, it's *time* that's the real currency of life, not money. If you ever need convincing of that fact then just remember that no matter how much bigger your current bank account gets, your current 'time' account is only getting smaller.

I've read some fantastic books devoted to improving performance. I recommend you take a look at them, especially *The Talent Code* by Daniel Coyle and *Bounce* by Matthew Syed. The fellas who've written these books are razor sharp... the sort of people that can watch a film like *The Matrix* or *Interstellar* without needing a running commentary. So, it might be a good idea to distil, in a few lines, what these great books are about.

It's a while since I read them so I'll give you the gist of what each author said. They both believe that talent is not born but is something which is created by practice. They explain that the more you practise, the more your performance improves.

Now you'll say to me *that's a load of cobblers Hingo, I spent four weeks solid revising Physics and I failed my Physics GCSE.* Right, well now comes the interesting bit. You see it's no good just doing any old practice and hoping it works; you have to practise in a certain way, otherwise you're just wasting time... and you don't want to be doing that after what I just said about time do you?

I'll give you an example. When I was revising (practising) for my Maths 'O' Level (now GCSE), I remember sitting down every morning of the Easter holidays trying to get a grip of the past papers that my dad had requested within about 15 minutes of reading my school report. Meanwhile, my mum would be busy at the back door getting rid of my mates (Millsy and Co.) who had come round to witness the unusual spectacle of someone they knew *actually* revising for an exam. In the end I got a 'C', which in those days was a bare pass, but I knew after the exam that I hadn't prepared properly. I wasn't practising (revising) in the right way.

What *I* was doing was making a half-hearted attempt to answer the questions. You know, just reading the question and thinking "Vectors, no problem, I can do that" and then flitting onto the next question after answering the easy bits. The problem was that it just seemed too much like hard work to sit at the dining room table (we did like to eat our dinner in style) and bash out the full answer to each question.

What I should have been doing was engaging in something called 'deep practice'. This is a phrase that Coyle uses in his book to describe practising at the edge of your comfort zone. In the example of those maths papers above, deep practice would have been trying to answer the questions *fully* but in my own time. And it's deep practice which apparently has an effect on the circuitry in your nervous system which produces the improvement.

Now you might argue that I *was* improving because at least I was trying to answer *some* of the questions which were likely to come up in the examination and to that extent you would be right. However, when you're trying to be good at something, it's not so much improvement but the *rate of improvement* that counts. Essentially it means that it's the speed at which you're improving that matters. Therefore, you have to respect how you spend your time. So, as I mentioned above, I was doing the right of sort of 'practise' by having a go at past exam questions, it's just that instead of trying to answer the full question I was just tackling the first few easy bits of the question (parts a and b), before sloping off to play knock-and-run with Millsy.

Syed's thoughts on practice, which he describes as purposeful practice, are that improvement comes from feedback and the most valuable feedback comes from failure. Going back to my Maths revision above, if I had tried to answer the difficult parts of the question say c, d and e, I would have been getting the answers wrong which would have encouraged me to find out why I was getting them wrong before striving to get them right.

Trying to answer those maths questions fully and quietly under non-exam conditions was the way forward. I did eventually manage to learn this lesson and my subsequent Maths results got gradually better and better as a result, but not before I'd passed through the exit door of the second expensive school.

So to sum up, in order to maximise the time spent practising:

1. Focus on specific areas that you know will lead to an improvement (such as past papers).

2. Practise at the edge of your capability so that you are making mistakes (try and answer *all* parts of the question).

3. Use the feedback from each mistake to improve.

Rani's Top Tip – It's not improvement that counts, it's the rate of improvement and that means deep practice.

PART THREE

WHAT DO YOU NEED TO DO TO BE GOOD AT ANYTHING?

CHAPTER 12

Lose the fear of failure

When I was a kid praise hadn't been invented. My parents, like most others, were avid readers of that infamous book *The 1970s Guide to Parenting,* which states on page 127 section (ii)

"Whatever you do... always remember to criticise your child's best efforts".

And section (ii) went on to state

"...if that doesn't make them feel truly shit then never forget to reinforce the message that any form of failure makes them a failure."

I remember once coming home from school with a big grin on my face and I said "Dad, I came top in French Comprehension at school?"

"What mark did you get?"

"I got 75%, Dad".

"75%! So let me get this straight, you lost 25% of the marks and you're celebrating?"

"Err... something like that Dad, yes."

This was the level of encouragement at home, so what about school?

At school, I started off being good at English, coming first or second in a class out of about 35. Then I got one dreadful mark of 19% for an essay titled *The*

Sinking Dinghy which, in fairness to the teacher, was probably worth 19% but stay with me on this. So, what happened was, my teacher said to me something like, "Well Neil, English never was your strongest subject." For the rest of my schooldays I reinforced this belief by telling anyone that cared to ask that "I'm crap at English." and of course delivering poor grades. Does this sound familiar? I thought it would.

Can you think of a better way of instilling fear into a child than the two examples above? On the one hand, I was made to feel like a failure for bombing in a single essay and on the other I was made to feel like a failure even when I *had* succeeded in French Comprehension. This set me up perfectly for a debilitating fear of failure for the next 20 years.

Now I don't blame my parents, my teachers or the monster that lives under my bed for this sort of nurturing, because pretty much everyone was brought up like this when I was young. I imagine that 20 years before that it was even worse. The message I got as a child was simply that if you fail at something, then *you* are a failure. What no-one taught me when I was at school was the principle that failure is the most important ingredient for success. How else are you supposed to learn? When things go well, the only message you get it is to keep doing the same thing. But when things go wrong, that's when you start to dissect your performance and it's this analysis that helps you explore all sorts of ways to improve. Something you would never have done had you succeeded.

Right, we've established that it's important to fail but

what you need to know is how do you lose the fear of failure? Well, first of all I think what you have to do is establish what it is you're scared of. Are you scared of not succeeding, really? Are you scared of losing money? Are you scared of not being able to speak a language properly? Really, are you scared of these things? I don't think so. So where does the fear come from? I'll tell you where it comes from. You're scared of what other people will think of you if you do fail. Does that sound like what you might really be scared of? I thought so. If you're ever in any doubt about that, think about where the fear came from in the first place. It was criticism... from other people!

Do you ever hear of a businessman who loses a fortune and then spends the rest of his life suffering from depression? So, a businessman might have £20 million in the bank one day and then have nothing the next day. What do you think is causing his depression... starving to death? I doubt it, this country won't let you starve... so he's still got food to eat. Nowhere to live? Again, probably not because if he's smart enough to build a fortune of £20 million he's probably going to be sharp enough to get a council house pretty quick. His basic needs are going to be met. So, what's the problem? He's lost face. That's it! He looks a bit of an idiot... so after much consideration, what he's going to do is spend the rest of his life punishing himself. An excessive response to the problem you may think.

Now let's just change the storyline a bit. If you said to this businessman "you have a serious problem with your arm and it's going to cost exactly £20 million to undertake this state-of-the-art surgery, which has only been carried out successfully three times before". What do you think he's going to say? Do you think he's going to say "Spend twenty million pounds on a shitty arm... at that price you can cut it off mate?" He's not, is he? Now it turns out the operation is a success, the surgeons have saved his arm but he is 20 million quid worse off. Do you think he's going to feel depressed because he's £20 million worse off? I doubt it very much, do you? He probably feels elated, but essentially, he's in the same place as if he'd lost £20 million at the roulette wheel. A healthy body with no money. It's just that in the second scenario he doesn't look like an idiot and *other people's perspective of him is totally different.* His friends are saying that this wise sensible man has spent a fortune on repairing his arm and it has worked, not "how did that mug blow £20 million... what a muppet!"

All right then... if I'm so clever what's the answer? How do you get over the fear of what people think about you? The answer is, you have to be able to laugh at yourself.

Allow me to elaborate. One of the most frightening things that a person can do is to speak in public. Go on, think about it. It's quite scary isn't it? This is something I have to do quite a bit and, although I can give you lots of good advice, the key to making a good speech is the ability to laugh at yourself. That's it. Yes, that really is it. But my word, is that a hard thing for some people to do?

Laughing at yourself is the best way to take the pressure off yourself because from my experience there's no better way to get an audience on your side. This doesn't mean you have to make a complete dick of yourself, but if you do trip over in front of your audience, don't pretend that nothing's happened, because then you will look like a dick. This is the same in day-to-day life. People will warm to you if you don't take yourself too seriously and laugh at yourself now and again. It also takes the pressure off *them* having to be perfect.

Rani's Top Tip – Be prepared to laugh at yourself now and again. It takes the pressure off your performance.

CHAPTER 13

Make consistently good decisions

This seems as good a time as any for a chapter on decision making. It seems to me that successful people are the ones who are always making good decisions.

When I was about 9 years old, I remember watching *Midlands Today* and there was a bloke on TV who specialised in eating lightbulbs. Yes, eating lightbulbs. He ate the whole thing. He'd break the glass and eat that first, then he would eat the filament in the middle and then he would finish off with that metal bit on the bottom. I can't quite remember whether it was a screw in lightbulb or a push fitting that he preferred but then again, I imagine his palate wasn't overly fussy after being subjected to half a kilo of broken glass. I remember him wearing a suit as well. Can you imagine that, wearing a suit to dine out on a lightbulb? Now that is class! When the presenter asked him whether he wanted another one his eyes lit up. No, they didn't. I'm sorry.

Now I'm not saying that I was one of the world's brightest kids (I promise that's the last one) but even at the age of nine, I could see that eating lightbulbs was unlikely to be good for him. Eating a lightbulb looked to me like a bad decision. Eating two lightbulbs looked like two bad decisions.

If you're always making good decisions then you're moving closer to your target. Think about your life as a game of snakes and ladders with your goal sitting at square 100. Every good decision gets you up a ladder and every bad decision lets you slide down a snake. You won't need anyone else to tell you if you're making bad decisions because you'll be hovering around box 19. Look around you. People who make consistently good decisions are doing well and people who make consistently bad decisions are doing badly. I'm afraid that if you're making bad decisions then it's not a coincidence that you're struggling to reach your goal. I mean, how can eating lightbulbs on any level be a good decision unless, I suppose, you want to be England's Number One lightbulb eater.

Another example of a poor decision would be to say, borrow your mother's new Volkswagen Scirocco GTX when she's on holiday in Majorca and leave it somewhere dodgy so that the car gets nicked, smashed up and burnt out. So that when you pick her up from the airport and she asks if there's any news, you know that pretty soon there'll be a major bollocking coming your way. And let me tell you this, nobody can dole out a bollocking like my mum... just ask Millsy!

When I was younger, I seemed to have a real talent for making bad decisions so I went to see my dad for a bit of advice. He was an Ear, Nose and Throat Surgeon, so you can imagine how calm and chilled out he had to be in order to make good decisions under pressure (we'll forget about the photocopier for now). I asked him how he reacted when faced with difficult choices in those situations. He gave me a great piece of advice and that was, 'when you need to make a decision, take your time'. What he meant by this was, take your time to think through your options.

Have you ever been in an interview, been asked a question and then immediately blurted out the answer? Well, I'll tell you something. If you had just waited one second before answering, you would have given a different answer. If you had waited two seconds before answering, you would have given a better answer. But if you had waited a whole three seconds before answering, you would have been awarded a Nobel Prize for your answer. So, remember that whenever you're asked an important question, give yourself a few moments to think before you decide what you're going to say.

This advice works in virtually any circumstances you can think of, even Formula 1, where time is something you haven't got a right lot of. Michael Schumacher never had the fastest reaction times so I'm told, but what he did have was the ability to *anticipate* trouble on the circuit. This allowed him a few more moments to think and the result was good decisions... oh yes and a not too shabby *seven World Championship titles.*

Every single minute of every day you're making decisions, even now you're making a decision. Shall I carry on reading this book or shall I nip downstairs and fix myself a nice piece of toast with raspberry jam?

That's a decision, not a very difficult one, but it's still a decision. So, to sum up, when you're making a decision:

1. Take your time to consider your options.

2. Decide on one option.

3. Execute it

Once you've made your decision, get on with it, that way if you've made the wrong one, you can change your mind and take another option without wasting too much time. That's why the only bad decisions are the ones which aren't made. Remember that.

Rani's Top Tip – When you need to make a decision, take your time. But when you've made it, get on with it.

CHAPTER 14

Stop comparing yourself with other people

If you want to feel truly shit about yourself, then comparing yourself with others is probably the number one way of going about it. For about 99% of my life, I compared myself with other people. I think it came from my parents, who used to compare me with one of my best mates who's called Slacker. For the record, he wasn't actually a slacker but he had an allergic reaction to a BCG injection and he had about a year off school so the name stuck. Anyway, my parents forever used to say "Why are you always in trouble and coming bottom of the class?" and then I'd wait for the immortal words that every bollocking would end in "Why can't you be more like Slacker?" Slacker made a cracking joke about this when he was best man at my wedding, as well as doing an impersonation of my dad, which I thought was a great effort.

Let me set the scene. Slacker was like the perfect son my parents never had. I think he liked hanging around with me because it gave his troublemaking side an airing. Now before you start worrying about the Slack man getting into trouble, you can relax, because he never did. There was an unwritten agreement between us. The essence of it could be summed up in a single incident. If *we* stole McVities Chocolate Digestives from the school kitchen at 11.30pm at night, then *I* alone would take the can for it.

In front of my parents, Slacker's performances merited BAFTA nomination. He would stifle multiple yawns as he listened to my mum's story about raising someone from the dead, whilst sipping his beer at such a slow rate that he made my dad look like a hell raiser. I mean, if he was auditioning for the role of perfect son, I'd have sacked myself and given him the job. The great thing about Slacker is that I never resented him for the way my parents compared me with him because he is such a top bloke. It must have been hard for them to see him cruising through school on auto pilot while I was experiencing problems with both engines and looking for somewhere to ditch.

I'm sure you can identify with being on the receiving end of an unfair comparison at some stage of your life. I don't honestly know the real reason we compare ourselves to others. Maybe it's something that comes from childhood, or it's just something that comes naturally to us when we feel it's about time we gave ourselves some serious punishment. But let me tell you something. It's got to be one of the most disempowering things you can possibly do and I'll tell you for why. Whenever you compare yourself with somebody you only compare the single item where you perceive the other person to be better than you. So, you might say, he's got more money than me, she's better looking than me... you never for one moment say well I'm better at football than him and *she* eats like a pig. What you do is take that little bit where someone is superior to you and you just smash yourself with it. Does this sound familiar? Ignoring every single one of your positives and then honing in on that one negative and destroying yourself with it? I used to do this a lot as a kid and no I didn't have many hobbies before you ask.

Okay so now we have defined the problem, what's the solution? It's not easy to just switch off from that negative behaviour. Well... what you have to do is consider yourself to be an annual set of accounts or achievements which probably works better.

In this set of achievements, you might have various categories (in no particular order) such as:

1. Money earned per annum
2. Level of fitness
3. Relationship with partner
4. Quality of relationships in general
5. Mental and physical health
6. Hobbies
7. Fun/holidays/places travelled to.

And each year you just compare yourself with your previous year's performance under each heading. The idea then is that you're comparing *yourself* only with *yourself.* NOW THAT'S A FAIR COMPARISON *and* it doesn't drain your energy. And do you know what? If all that fails, ask yourself; do I really want to be that person I'm comparing myself with because I'd be amazed if your answer to that question is actually 'yes'.

Rani's Top Tip – Comparing yourself with yourself is the only fair comparison you can make.

CHAPTER 15

Build yourself
a support system

In order to succeed, you must have people around you *who want you* to succeed.

Whenever you're trying to be good at something, or achieve something, your efforts will be subject to the scrutiny of those around you. What you'll find is that some of your friends and family will be supportive and others will not. The skill is working out who is on your side. Those people you can confide in. "Ah…" but you say to me, "these people are my friends, they must be on my side, this person is in my family, of course he is my friend, what are you talking about?"

Whilst it's true that your real friends and most of your family will be on your side, there will also be people close to you who are envious of you and want you to fail. An old friend of mine once confided in me his deepest fear with this one immortal line: *'Every time one of my friends succeeds, a little part of me dies'*. He's obviously not the sort you'd want as a Sherpa when you're trying to climb Everest but at least, I suppose, he would be an honest one. He's the sort that could look you in the eye while he's cutting the rope.

One of my friends is called Gob (you'll understand if you meet him). When I was starting in business in 1996 he was working in the City. His first ever bonus was two hundred and fifty thousand pounds, which made him considerably richer than me, and he lent me the full amount. As acts of friendship go, that wasn't too shabby because, I'll be honest with you, in 1996 I don't think I would have lent me two hundred and fifty quid. Anyway, I must think about repaying that money sometime. But back to Gob in a minute.

Over the years, I have lost a number of friends through natural causes, the majority of these causes were that these people simply did not have my best interests at heart (and still don't). They wanted deep down, well not even deep down it was probably quite high on their agenda, to see me fail spectacularly and eventually I worked out who these people were. However, so that you don't start culling half decent people for the sake of it, it might be a good idea to take a look at the definition of a friend.

The dictionary definition of the word friend is: *'A person who is not an enemy or opponent; an ally'.*

Now ask yourself, how many of your friends are really allies? My definition of a friend is a bit better than the one in the dictionary. I define a friend as 'someone who has your best interests at heart'. Think about that for a moment... it's pretty difficult for someone to have your best interests at heart and not be your friend.

That's not to say friends are not allowed to take the piss out of you, because that is essential. But there are certain friends who can *only* take the piss out of you and can never say one supportive comment. What these people do is take your energy. The energy you need to be good at something, these people take it from you with their constant sniping and give you nothing in return. That's why you need to get rid of them.

The path of friendship does not always run smooth, even with my good friend Gob. I remember one night in the early '90s we rolled in from the Lazy Fox and sat down to begin a discussion on the relative merits and demerits of the footballer John Barnes. Within moments of the debate commencing, furniture was flying, glasses were broken and pictures were falling off the wall. The exchange of views was interrupted by my sister (who, can you believe it, lived downstairs from Gob and came upstairs to find out what was going on) at the point where my head was being crushed into the sports section of the *Daily Telegraph*. The strange thing about me and Gob is that every time we have a fight, verbal or physical, it seems to bring us closer together.

You also need to remember that a lot of good friendships take time to establish. You have good times and bad times, so you can't just write a relationship off over a minor incident like the one above. Having said that, when you do realise that someone actually isn't a friend, you don't need to have a big bust up. You can just do what I call 'The English Fallout'. If you look in the *Oxford English Dictionary*, it is defined as 'ceasing contact with a person and, on the occasions you meet, pretend to be their friend'.

This sounds a good way of getting rid of someone doesn't it? The reason I like this method is because when you fall out with someone there is a certain pressure to fall back in again and you don't really want to fall back in because you don't really want to be friends. The English Fallout allows you to drift apart gently. That way the bonds of 'friendship' are allowed to break gradually, but more importantly, permanently.

When you're younger, you tend to feel under pressure to be friends with cool and trendy people and by doing this you can miss out on real friends who are on your doorstep. Allow me to introduce you to Roy. He runs a timber yard from the house next door to me. Roy manages operations from a 'favela'-styled construction at the rear of his garden, beside which he is growing a Ford Sierra. He's often accompanied by his beautiful black Labrador, Monty, whose loyalty is such that he simply refuses to go the bathroom anywhere but our front garden. On the days when Roy is not busy devaluing our property, he can be found deep in his shanty town with his mate Charlie, running an illegal cider-making operation. It's good stuff as well... very dry, just how I like it. But, I'll tell you something, if you were to knock on Roy and Liz's door at 11.30pm on a Sunday night with some obscure request, they would have a gin and tonic in your hand within 3.2 seconds of opening the door, along with that half a kilo of naturally occurring Uranium 238 you asked for.

If you're struggling to work out who is a friend and who is not, then just consider how you feel after you've been with them. After seeing them, do you generally feel energised and in good spirits and ready to persevere with your chosen challenge, or do you feel like you want to give up? If it's the latter then there's a good chance they're not your friend.

Rani's Top Tip – A friend is someone who has your best interests at heart.

CHAPTER 16

Get organised

When I was studying at Birmingham Polytechnic in 1989, I got a holiday job working for St Modwen Developments. I only got the job because my dad knew the chairman. I think he'd taken his tonsils out or something, which I suppose is one way of getting a job when you need one. Anyway, while I was there, I was put under the watchful eye of a guy called Jimmy. Jimmy was the superstar of the office and, to make me feel great, he was only two years older than me (and still is as far as I am aware), with a nice comfy seat on the board of directors. I wasn't even in my final year at polytechnic (see, there I was, comparing myself – naughty).

Jimmy's favourite saying was 'organisation is the key to success.' I remember being fascinated by his desk. Everything was meticulously laid out, with box files of major projects set out at one end and agreements for lease at the other. The middle of the desk itself had been built like a cockpit with Jimmy surrounded by nine in-trays containing letters and correspondence stacked neatly around him. Tray one contained contracts for signature whilst tray nine was more of an overflow for the bin. Each tray filled up with letters on a daily basis (this was in the days before email) and each day, trays one to seven were emptied in order of priority. Even the *drawers* of his desk looked like they'd been hoovered on a daily basis because, on closer inspection, there wasn't a crumb of food in sight. Quite an achievement when you consider he was in charge of the office biscuit tin. It was only when I sat at his desk while he was on holiday that it dawned on me that just maybe he had a point about organisation and success.

Jimmy was smart enough to know that time was the real currency of life and any activity that involved wasting it, was analysed, dismantled and then rebuilt accordingly. I am just Googling his name now and the first item I see is a headline which details him purchasing a chain of hotels for a tidy £700 million. I suggest you read the last sentence again if you still don't think there's a connection between organisation and success.

Right then, let's take a peek at the other end of the organisation spectrum. I've got a mate called Brian and his office looks as if an artic carrying oversized steel sections has been driven through it and then reversed back out for good measure. From the office he runs a little property business but he has one problem. His problem is simple. He is completely disorganised. There'll be a letter from his Aunt Hilda, an invoice from Kwik Fit, three bank statements, a letter about the kids' school uniform and an invitation to a party all in the same pile. It's a disaster. Every time I go to his house it causes me physical pain when I calculate the amount of time that he incinerates looking for things. It takes him ten minutes minimum to find anything. The thing is that whenever I see him, I can't resist asking him some sort of detailed question "Eh Brian, you couldn't tell me how much rent you're charging on 3 Geary's Lane?" He'll say, "Yes mate, give us a minute". And of course, ten minutes later he's swearing like a docker and ferreting through his filing cabinet. Can't find the rent. He then jumps onto the computer and I can see all his files sprawled out in one random documents folder.

At the point I mention the idea about putting a bit of system in place, the reaction I get, blimey you'd think I'd been on a date with his mother. Give me one minute and I'll explain to you *why* it's important to be organised. Let's say Brian has 30 properties and on Monday he goes out and buys another one, that's 31. He contacts a new managing agent to look after the latest property because he has no other properties in that part of the city. Brian asks the managing agent what his fees are and the managing agent says 10% of the rent. Brian has a feeling that's expensive but because he can't be bothered to go through the torture of searching through his files to compare it with what he's paying the other agents, he just accepts 10% and puts the phone down.

If Brian was organised, he could check his files and immediately see that in some cases his fees are as low as 7% of the rent. If the rent for the latest property was £500 per month then that 3% saving (10% minus 7%) would equate to a saving of £15 per month which is £180 over the year and that is for something which should take two minutes to check. Think about it, that's two minutes work to save £180 which in my mind is the same as earning £180. I don't know about you but I'll happily work for £90 quid a minute. All Brian needed to do to save that money was to be able to access his files.

Have you ever heard of that expression 'the devil is in the detail'? Well, it means that if you don't pay attention to little details then you may run into problems. The situation here is that if, like Brian, you're not organised you can't even *see* the detail. And if you can't see the detail then you can't attend to it which leads to problems. Attention to detail in any activity is the bit which allows you to improve.

Right then, we've established that lack of organisation causes three things:

1. It wastes time

2. It prevents you from seeing the detail...

3. ...and if you can't see the detail, then you can't attend to it.

That should be all the incentive you need to get organised in your mission to be good at something.

Rani's Top Tip – It's not very glamorous and it's not very cool, but organisation *is* the key to success.

CHAPTER 17

Learn to make an honest assessment of your own performance

Now you might be wondering back in Chapter 15 what on earth Gob could possibly have lent me that 250 grand for. Well, read on and you'll find out.

Over the years, I'd refurbished a few terraced houses, sold them and generally made some money on them, but not always. However, it seemed to me that the real profits were in building new houses. The trouble with new build was that the start-up costs were much higher. The upshot was that I needed 250 grand to build my first development and this is where Gob came in, who as it happens, had just received a 250-grand bonus from his job in the City. Who says timing isn't everything? However, there was one tiny problem. I'd never built a house before, which I am prepared to admit is not ideal preparation when you are about to spend £250,000 of someone else's money. That particular detail may have been omitted when I went to ask Gob for the money.

Fast forward to the development. Once I got on site it didn't take long for the main contractor to realise that he was dealing with a complete novice and, like any predator worth his salt, he was prepared to wait. His name was Big Fin, which was a coincidence as he spent most of the week circling me before going in for the kill at 4pm on a Friday.

Building that first house was like a crash course in humiliation. By the time I finished the job I was exhausted. I could only see the negatives, partly because they were rammed down my throat every day by my friends, (who I hadn't realised yet weren't actually my friends) and partly because I sold the first house for a healthy 50 grand less than it was worth. That still feels good today. For the jackpot, I was reminded of that mistake every single day while I was building the second house because, by some quirk of fate, the second plot of land I bought was sat right next to the first one! Nice touch. When the combined scheme was completed, it had gone over budget and taken four months longer than anticipated.

Instead of berating myself for the mistakes I made, what I should have done was make an honest assessment of the facts. What I mean by that is, examined what I had done right and what I done wrong. So, let's look at the facts:

What I had done wrong
1. The scheme went over budget on cost by 15%
2. The scheme was delivered four months late

What I had done right
1. The scheme was built to the correct specification
2. The scheme produced a 20% profit

The problem was, the experience crushed me and I gave up building houses from then onwards. I wasn't able to see what I had done right because I was too busy listening to everyone else telling me how useless I was.

Looking at this objectively some 20 years later, it seems that there are three items you need to consider when undertaking a construction project. The scheme needs to be:

a) Built on time

b) Built within budget

c) Built to the correct specification

Even though I had not delivered on items a) timescale and b) budget, my predicted gross profit on the scheme had only been reduced by 5%, thanks to a healthy dose of house price inflation. I had however delivered on item c) and getting the quality of the build right is probably the most important bit for a beginner. Add that to the amount I would have learnt in that period and you are looking at a success story. But I was so beat up about it, I asked Big Pete Elliott to teach me how to become a bricklayer, because I was never going to make it as a house builder! What a way to think? Anyway, enough of the poor me. What did I learn from the experience? Now we're talking.

What I should have done at the end was this. Make an honest assessment of what I had done right and what I had done wrong, as above. What I *actually* did was to magnify all the things I did wrong and ignore all the things I got right. Does that sound familiar?

After carrying out the assessment of what I had done right and wrong, I *should* then have done two things:

I. Congratulated myself for doing the things I got right

II. Accepted the things I had got wrong and learnt from them

In any negative experience in life, there are two by-products. One is the emotion of the experience, which is normally a pretty shit one (or else it wouldn't be a negative experience would it?), the other is the little nuggets of gold, which are the lessons you have learnt. The skill is to take the gold and leave the emotion... after you've got drunk and smashed the place up of course.

Rani's Top Tip – The secret of any experience is to remember the lessons you've learnt and leave the emotion behind.

CHAPTER 18

Get your attitude into shape

When I had clinical depression back in '94 I bust a gut to try and get back on my feet. I did everything the doctors and psychiatrists told me. Anyway, after doing the exercises and relaxations and taking the drugs (medicinal not recreational), I tried to find a long-term solution to cure my depression. I searched and searched and searched for a single piece of wisdom that would help me get better... and believe it or not I found it. After reading over two hundred self-help books and biographies here is the gold and never forget it:

Positive people are generally happier and more successful than negative people.

Get these words tattooed onto your heart and read them every day (you may need to use a mirror). Once I worked this out, and it took a while, I changed my attitude overnight. From then on, I was determined to be the most positive person that walked on Planet Earth and I still try to be. Now I'm fully aware that the whole world and his dog are forever talking about positive attitude but nobody really explains what it means and why it's important. Allow me.

First of all, what do I mean by a positive attitude? Simple, for me a positive attitude means an expectation of a positive outcome. It means lots of other things of course but this is as good a definition as any. Basically, expecting something good to happen and not something bad.

The second thing is, why is it important? This is a bit more interesting and to answer the question I'm going to tell you a story. Some years ago, as I walked in the door from work one night, I picked up a letter and knowing that it was an invoice from my electricity supplier (who also happened to be my gas supplier) expected a bill for around £120. However, not only was there an invoice for £122.35 but also an additional invoice for £835.56 which sat innocently in the envelope behind the first invoice. You see, what happened in the olden days, before smart meters were invented, was that electricity companies used to estimate your readings to make it easier to invoice you because it saved them the trouble of visiting your house. Then, every now and again they would go to your house to read the meter, calculate the real bill and you'd have to pay the balance or receive a credit. The only problem was that this company hadn't read the meter for six years (I must think about applying for a job there sometime).

So, what happens next?

Scenario 1:

Let's say, I'm tired and hungry because I've just walked in from work and am feeling a bit negative. This is my thinking:

1. I expect that I'll have to pay this additional bill, it is a utility company after all and who gets away with not paying their electricity bill?

2. I am now worried because I can't afford it.

3. I know... I will ring the payment line right now and put the total amount on my credit card which is already suffering from severe chest pains.

4. Result – Good news: I don't owe the electricity supplier £835.56. Bad news: I owe the credit card company a further £835.56.

5. Outcome – Negative.

When you have a negative attitude then there is a negative expectation of the outcome. This negative expectation is what creates worry and when you are worried it's very difficult to think clearly. Have you ever tried to think clearly about something when you're panicking? Well worry is just a lesser form of panicking. As a result of your inability to think, you start to make poor decisions and poor decisions lead to poor results like the one above.

Scenario 2:

I see the bill and make a decision to leave it until the next morning. I get up the next morning, the sun is shining and I feel refreshed after hoovering up a nice bowl of Coco Pops for breakfast. I'm feeling positive and ready to deal with this utility bill. I am *now* thinking:

1. I expect that somehow I'll manage to wangle my way out of paying this bill.

2. I'm feeling relaxed because I'm thinking of the time when I managed to fluke my way onto Business Class to New York with the wife... not a bad one!

3. I know... I'll see if there's a negotiating position I can use that will help reduce the bill, like threatening to change suppliers for both electricity *and gas* if they charge me.

4. Result – Utility Company waive the invoice in full and apologise. I accept their apology with just a hint of a grin on my face.

5. Outcome – Positive.

Same scenario with completely different outcome.

Hopefully the story above shows you the importance of having a positive attitude as opposed to a negative one. When you have a positive attitude then there is an expectation of a positive outcome. You're expecting something good to happen so you're feeling relaxed. And when you're relaxed you're able to think clearly. Your ability to think helps you make good decisions, and good decisions lead to good results. Think about how many situations in your life which have produced a negative outcome but could have produced a positive one *if* you had been able to think through the problem.

So why, you may ask, are positive people generally happier and more successful than negative people? The answer my friend is that positive people make good decisions and good decisions lead to a happy and successful life; this is why a positive attitude is important.

Rani's Top Tip – Positive thinking leads to a positive outcome.

CHAPTER 19

Learn how to think

In the previous chapter we worked out that a positive attitude allowed you to relax and this enabled you to think through a situation resulting in a good decision. We also saw that when you're worried, this shuts down your ability to think and this generally results in a poor decision. Let me show you the difference between what's happening when you're worrying and when you're thinking.

Just for a moment, consider that there are two sections in your brain: the subconscious part and the conscious part. When you're *worrying* about something, the material is lying in the conscious part of your brain and you're pulling the problem in all sorts of directions. You never leave the problem alone to sort itself out because you're constantly tugging at it and as a result, the problem doesn't get solved.

Thinking is different to *worrying*. Thinking doesn't actually mean thinking about something all the time. It means thinking about something and then forgetting about it and then having another little think and then forgetting about it again. It's all very relaxed. A bit like doing a crossword while you're having an afternoon snooze. The important bit about thinking is *not thinking*. I know that sounds a bit strange but when you're not thinking there is actually something else that's doing the thinking for you and that's called your subconscious brain. Unlike the conscious brain which is analytical and likes to take problems apart, and is very good at it, the subconscious brain specialises in coming up with solutions. You need both parts of the brain but most of us tend to give the complete job of problem solving to the conscious brain.

In your mission to be good at something, you need to learn to trust your subconscious brain to work out a solution to the problem you're encountering. The subconscious brain likes you to leave him alone. He's a bit like a mardy solicitor when you're trying to buy a house and you're ringing him up every day to see if you've exchanged contracts. The subconscious brain doesn't like to be interrupted because he operates much better if he's left in peace. So, if you're tempted to contact him before he's ready to give you an answer, he's likely to pick up the phone and go "You again... can't you see I'm dealing with it, you blithering idiot... I'll get back to you when I'm ready?"

Now I'm going to tell you something important here, something very important, because when I understood how the system worked it changed my life. In a situation where I need some advice, I'll say something like "Subconscious Brain, I'm not quite sure whether I should jack my job in to become a professional drummer but I'll wait for a day or two to get your advice". Sometimes the subconscious brain needs a day or so to get back to you and other times you will get an answer within minutes which was the case with my question above.

"Neil, thank you for your call this morning. I have considered this career in... drumming I think it was, and in the light of your current financial circumstances:

1. Three mortgages totalling £325,000

2. Two credit cards with a combined debt of £8,100

3. And a current overdraft £6,370,

I am not entirely convinced that it is a suitable profession to satisfy your existing financial requirements and therefore my final answer is no... you *bloody* fool".

It might seem ridiculous, but this is exactly how it works. I normally leave a caseload of items with my subconscious brain in the evening or just before I go to bed and then I normally get a call from him when I'm in the shower the next morning with a list of good decisions that I am going to make that day... like looking for a real job. It's as simple as that.

Rani's Top Tip – The secret of problem solving is to *stop worrying*. Just ask your subconscious brain for the solution and wait until he gets back to you.

CHAPTER 20

Learn to become a positive person

From the last couple of chapters, you can hopefully see the effect that being a positive person can have on your ability to be good at something, so your next question should be "How do I become a positive person?" Well, thankfully this is the easy bit. You don't need to have been born a positive thinking person or brought up by positive people, but I'm not going to lie, these factors do make it easier. Here's a little list of things you can do to get you started:

1) Get your work/life balance sorted – An excess of either work or dossing will lead to stress.

2) Look after your body – Try and keep out of The Greyhound say two nights a week.

3) Spend time nurturing your relationships – Don't look for a scrap where there isn't one (one of my personal challenges).

4) Diet – There's a link between what you eat and how you feel... amazingly!

5) Learn to breathe properly – This helps you sleep properly (something I'm actually *very* good at).

6) Talking positively – This is the one that changes your life.

The first five items in this list can be attended to straightaway and these will have an immediate effect in terms of feeling positive. But I want to focus on number six on the list because the rest of them you can probably sort out without my help.

Talking positively is the most important step in thinking positively. Have you ever heard of that phrase neuro linguistic programming? Yes? No? I'm asking you a question here! Well, that's just a fancy way of saying that your brain believes what your mouth tells it. That's all. Here's an example of how it works.

Over the years, one of my least favourite subjects was IT which is short for Information Technology (for anyone over 40, this translates as computing). Anyway, in order to qualify as a lecturer, I had to pass an exam called a Post Graduate Certificate in Higher Education and one of the modules was called *Supporting Learning with Technology*. The lecturer was pretty slack and, when all the laptops were out, as long as Panos and I synchronised our nodding, she didn't notice us watching the Champions League highlights on ITV catch up from the night before. (Thirty years after leaving school and I'm *still* acting the goat in lessons… pathetic!).

Anyway, when the module was introduced, I remember hearing myself say, "not IT, I'm cobblers at this". Hearing myself say these words immediately alerted me to my negative behaviour. And, having made a decision to cop on to myself, I thought I would try a little experiment. I'd heard about this neuro linguistic stuff and I thought I would give it a go. So I started praising myself by saying "Neil... you are the absolute business at this IT. You do know it's an absolute piece of cake don't you?" and then, "I don't where you get this amazing talent from, but I tell you something old son, you are an absolute legend on the black box." I was feeding my brain with all this bull... but wait for it... the best bit was that my brain hoovered it all up. My brain believed everything I'd told it. Before I knew it, I had got 'A's in all parts of the module and more importantly I do actually believe now that IT *is* a piece of cake.

Even though I was pleased with my results on the module, I lost a little bit of respect for my brain after that. I was amazed that it could be so gullible. How could an organ with the capability of managing the entire operating system of the space shuttle using only 6% of its capacity succumb to flattery? But it did. And while we're on the subject of the Space Shuttle, you probably didn't know that my Uncle Roop was involved with building the internal structure. So don't blame him for those dodgy heat resistant ceramic tiles that fell off. He had nothing to do with them.

Hopefully that little story shows you how simple it is to think positively about any subject you find difficult. It all starts with talking positively. From my own experience it's much better if you can talk out loud so you can actually hear your own words, as opposed to talking to yourself in your head. To really drill the message home, talk out loud while you're looking at yourself in the mirror. That's even more powerful. But most importantly keep repeating to yourself day after day how good you are. Don't just say it in a monotone boring way. It works much better if you put some emotion into it like I did, "Crikey Hingo, when it comes to computing... you are the man". The more emotion that went in, the more I started to believe that I was good at IT. I started having a go at all sorts of PowerPoint presentations and fancy Excel spreadsheets. Seeing the results of my work reinforced the belief and removed my fear of IT forever.

The point is that you need to train yourself to speak differently *about* yourself and *to* yourself. It's an easy thing to do. Every time you hear yourself saying something negative about your talents just stop and say "Hold on I was being a tad negative there. Let me just rephrase that..."

At home, I don't go mad at my kids for swearing. They're part Irish after all and are therefore genetically programmed to swear. However, if I do hear them say "I can't do this" or "it's impossible" or "there's no way" that's when they get a proper telling off and I'll tell you for why. Swearing is just naughty words, nothing more. Words like 'can't' or 'impossible' destroy people's lives and extinguish people's dreams. So folks, be mindful of the real bad language next time little Johnny tells you he's only going to the effing shops.

Rani's Top Tip – If you want to start thinking positively, then start talking positively.

PART FOUR

PUTTING IT ALL TOGETHER

CHAPTER 21

I threw a stone to hit a rock

In the first three parts of the book, I've given you the essential information on how to be good at anything. In order to help you see how close you already are to being good at anything *and* remember this essential information, I split it into:

PART ONE: What are you *already good at*?

PART TWO: What do you need to *know* to be good at anything?

PART THREE: What do you need to *do* to be good at anything?

Sitting in the chapters within these parts, lies the formula for being good at anything. But before I tell you what that formula is, I'm going to tell you where and how it was built... read on amigo!

I normally go on holiday to a place in south-east Spain called Mojacar. It's a small town on the Costa de Almeria to be precise, and I've spent many great holidays there with my mum and dad and then later with my own family. I like it because the atmosphere in the town is very relaxed. You don't have to dress up to go out and you can walk into most restaurants with wet sand squelching out of your flip flops (don't try it at La Cabaña or my mate Jorge will give you the look) which I suppose is a big factor for me in terms of choosing a relaxing holiday destination.

If you take a leisurely stroll along the seafront, you'll eventually reach the Hotel Indalo. You'll recognise it because it's the only building with more than four storeys. When it was built, it was rumoured that Thomson holidays had to pay a huge 'fine' to Mojacar Town Hall to avoid demolishing it because the maximum height of any building in the area is of course four storeys. Keep walking past the Hotel Indalo and you'll find yourself on a coastal pathway at the edge of the Indalo Mountain. It's a beautiful walk because the path is high up and overlooks the sea, as well as being a great place to slope off from the wife and kids to have a little chill out time on your own. Now, as a kid one of the things I used to love to do was throw stones. Not at people I hasten to add, well not often anyway, but aiming at some sort of target... maybe a gatepost or a pillar, that sort of thing.

I usually stop in the same place to admire the view on my favourite Spanish walk, but on this particular occasion, something drew me to an object in the water about ten metres below and 15 metres out to sea. The object turned out to be a rock but it was invitingly shaped like a parrot's head (not that I've got anything against parrots) and I felt a great temptation to start chucking stones to see if I could hit it.

After about five minutes I'd got quite close but still

I hadn't hit it. After a further five minutes I was even closer but still no joy. After 15 minutes *and* 20 minutes I'd got as close you get, but I'd *still* not hit it. This is where I would normally start swearing and cursing my bad luck, but it struck me that no external force could possibly be interested in such an unimportant pastime as me trying to hit a rock with a stone. I realised then that *I* was in control. There were no external forces influencing this non-event. It was just me and the rock, and the stone separating us. So, feeling slightly empowered, I thought I would try something else.

What I did was change the way I was throwing. I realised that I was throwing the stone in a random manner. I remembered some aiming technique that Millsy had shown me when we were kids lobbing stones at a gatepost and at the same time trying not hit the horses standing beside it. So, I started to *aim* my stones at the target. Initially my throws were overshooting the rock by a distance and then falling short then too much to the right, a wee bit to the left... but not for long. The upshot was that after a further 5 minutes I eventually hit the rock and then *kept* hitting it and hitting it. I hit it maybe three times out of every five throws.

Right then, what had I done that was so clever? Well, I spent a bit of time using trial and error, finding out in dead simple terms what was working and what wasn't.

It seemed that the overarm throwing technique was working along with my ability to select the right type of stones because my stones were *reaching* the target even though they were not actually hitting it.

At the same time, something wasn't right as I was

reaching the target but *never* actually hitting it. It turned out that I was not aiming the stones properly. After using my long forgotten aiming technique, with a few adjustments along the way, the stones began to hit the target consistently. After I had hit the rock a few times, I felt like I couldn't miss.

The feedback from each failed throw had allowed me to adjust the next throw. I came back from the walk reflecting on another wasted afternoon in the Life of Neil Hingorani. However, a couple of years later, I realised that what I'd been doing was following the core formula for succeeding at anything:

The Process of Success (The Process)

1. Have a go – Throw a stone.
2. Use trial and error – Keep throwing stones for a period of time but doing it a slightly different way each time (remember you may need to get worse to get better).
3. If it's working – Keep doing it – Throwing overarm and stone selection is working for me.
4. If it isn't working:
    a) Learn from your mistakes – I am still not hitting the target. The problem seems to me that I am not aiming the stone at the target, I am just throwing in the direction of the target and hoping. (The real gold in any experience is the lesson learnt).
    b) Leave the emotion behind – The reason I'm missing the target is because I haven't

thrown a stone for 20 years... not because I am the world's unluckiest person. Time to stop punishing myself.

5. As more things start working motivation increases – Throwing overarm and selecting the right stones is working for me. If I add this to my old aiming technique, then I am bound to hit the target.

6. Result – After making a few adjustments to my aiming technique, I hit the target and am able to do it consistently – Success.

About six months after the stone-throwing sojourn, I found that I was spending a lot more time working in Spain and as a result I needed to speak the language. After trying to do that in Birmingham, I eventually found myself at a Spanish language school in Granada. As the only surveyor in the third-floor balcony-style classroom with a major structural crack, I quickly recognised the importance of sitting in the section of the room which was least likely to land in the swimming pool beneath. Anyway, for some reason, I linked stone throwing to learning Spanish. Maybe the fact that it was hot, I was in Spain and overlooking an expanse of water might have had something to do with it.

So here are the similarities in The Process of throwing a stone and learning a language:

1. Have a go – Enrolled at Brasshouse College in Birmingham for evening classes with Nati Knight (who – stands back in amazement – had previously taught my wife Sophie at Sutton Girl's School).

2. Use trial and error – Tried different ways of learning to speak Spanish by listening to Spanish tapes in the car, watching Spanish films and speaking Spanish to Nati who had to restrain herself from throttling me on occasions.

3. If it's working keep doing it – Realised that the language was built around the verbs. Therefore, focused my work on the verbs and let the other words stick to them.

4. If it isn't working:

    a) Learn from your mistakes – Eventually realised that I needed to study in Spain to be able to speak good conversational Spanish.

    b) Leave the emotion behind – Refused to be disheartened by the fact that I was the weakest (sorry second weakest 17/18) student in the class in the Brasshouse and had to move down a class.

5. As more things start working motivation increases – Being forced to speak Spanish on a daily basis in Granada added to my knowledge of the written language, produced an immediate improvement.

6. Result – After two weeks in Granada, I was able to speak good conversational Spanish – Success.

Then it dawned on me that maybe, just maybe, this same process could be used to enable me to become good at anything. I decided that my next challenge would be to try my hand at public speaking. And before you can say 'wouldn't it be ironic to lecture at a university after being expelled from one?' I became a lecturer in Real Estate at the University of Wolverhampton. However, the difference between now and the previous two activities was that I was *expecting* to succeed because I trusted The Process. I knew it worked. Again the results were excellent. I was turning into Noddy bleedin' White here.

Just so there's absolutely no confusion about what The Process is, it can be written as follows:

The Process

1. Have a go.
2. Use trial and error.
3. If it works keep doing it.
4. If it isn't working:
    a) Learn from your mistakes.
    b) Leave the emotion behind.
5. As more things start working motivation increases.
6. Result – success.

Armed with The Process, you now have the power to be good at anything. I mean it. You might think therefore, that this is a logical place for the book to end. Well, you're right it is...but it doesn't end here. However, if I'm being completely honest with you, when I started writing the book, *I* thought it would end here. It doesn't end here for a very good reason. Read on. Isn't this exciting?

CHAPTER 22

The 'C' word

As you've read above, by attempting a number of different challenges, I worked out that in order to become good at anything, say a skill, it was necessary to use The Process.

However, the problem I'd experienced over the years was that, even though I'd been through The Process a number of times, for a variety of different skills, I didn't always perform to the best of my ability when a particular skill was put to the test.

For example, as a footballer, even though I was considered to be a good footballer and played well in training, I wouldn't always perform well in a match situation; it often depended on how I started the game. If I started well and put a few good tackles in I was fine, but if I started the game with a few mistakes, I found it difficult to recover from them and would quite often go on to have a bad game.

So, I started to investigate why some people went straight from being good at something to performing consistently (Noddy White), whilst others, after gaining a skill, were not able to perform consistently (Me). It wasn't too long before I came across the word that everyone uses but nobody seems to know what it actually means. The word is 'confidence'.

But, let's just focus on the word *perform* for a second. Obviously when you are building a skill you have to perform that skill but what I mean by perform, in order to explain confidence, is quite simply *performing in a competitive environment.* So, if you're a footballer that means playing in a match, as opposed to training; if you're learning a language it means talking to other Spanish people, as opposed to a painfully slow error-ridden conversation with your teacher.

Confidence is the magic potion which allows Asterix and many others to *perform* a skill to the best of their ability. The dictionary definition talks about having a belief or trust in yourself, which I suppose is what I expected to read. But that definition never really made much sense to me. Confidence to me was always more of a feeling. To be more specific it was about how I *felt* about my ability to perform a skill.

Let's just say that you have been through The Process and built yourself a skill as say a footballer. The result of this will be that you will be feeling confident about your ability to play football. Well done... that's great. However, let's also assume your ability to play football has *never* been tested in a competitive environment such as a match. As soon as you start to perform in your first match, your confidence will be tested.

So how do you avoid losing that confidence after you've missed three tackles, headed the ball into your own net and missed an open goal from five yards out?

This my friend, is a lot more straightforward than you might think.

First of all, there are three things you need to consider when you perform:

a) How confident people *think*

b) How confident people *behave*

c) How confident people *talk to themselves*

We'll look at these headings in the following chapters but let's just rewind for a moment. Do you remember the stone throwing episode I told you about in Chapter 21? Well, I forgot to mention that, just as I arrived back in the Irish Rover from throwing a stone and eventually hitting a rock, and was enjoying a pint of Guinness, who did I meet but your very good self (run with me on this). You joined in a conversation that I was having with Dave the barman about my cousin Martin, who'd escaped from the French Foreign Legion dressed as a woman, and turned out to be in Dave's class at school in Blackburn.

When I met you, I told you about my experience of throwing a stone to hit a rock and, by pure coincidence, you mentioned that you'd seen a street poster that morning advertising the *Southern Spain Mixed Open (Boys and Girls) Stone Throwing Competition,* which was being held in Mojacar Playa the very next week. On hearing your news, *I* was all set to enter the competition myself but I soon picked up from the conversation that you were not a very confident person, so I then asked "Why don't we both enter?" You said to me. "I couldn't possibly do that; it's years since I've thrown a stone" or words to that effect.

Anyway, the very next day, I gave you a few lessons and you were doing a great job. You were definitely a good stone thrower... even better than me. I also told you that I needed to go home urgently as we'd run out of tea bags. It was also an opportunity to check up on my offices which had been ransacked that morning. But you promised me that you would enter the competition anyway and do your best to win.

So, just to re-cap, the situation as it stands is that you've been coached by me for a few hours, followed The Process and you've now acquired the skill of being a good stone thrower. You know you are a good thrower because you've hit a target in the water five times on the trot which was situated a good ten metres away. However, you've never been truly tested as a stone thrower because you've never played anyone in a competitive situation. This is all about to change as you tentatively submit your entry for your first stone throwing competition.

THE SOUTHERN SPAIN MIXED OPEN
(Boys and Girls)
STONE THROWING COMPETITION RULES

1. All competitors must stand on the platform behind the white line.

   This is painted on a timber platform which is two metres above the sea. The targets are flat pancake shaped objects which are slightly raised above the sea water. They have an inner circle, a middle circle and an outer edge.

2. Any competitor that falls into the water will be disqualified on the basis that he or she was acting the goat in the first place.

3. Round One: All competitors have a total of 20 stones and must hit the target, which is located ten metres from the white line, five times to qualify for the second round.

4. Round Two: All competitors have a total of 20 stones and must hit the target, which is located 12.5 metres from the white line, five times to qualify for the Final.

5. The Final: Finalists have 20 stones each and the winner is the competitor who hits the 12.5 metre target the most times.

6. If two or more finalists are tied after 20 throws then a play-off ensues where the competitors throw in turn and the winner is the person who hits the target (12.5 metre) the highest number of times with five throws.

7. The umpire's word is final and cannot be questioned even if it appears that an appalling decision has been made.

8. During the competition, the fish and chip van, "Assalt and Battery" is out of bounds to all competitors.

   There are 36 entrants in total and each one is allowed five minutes' practice before the start. In the first two rounds, competitors throw simultaneously and each competitor has an umpire checking whether their individual target has been struck.

In the final and play-off there is a single umpire and each competitor takes it in turn to throw at the same target.

The Process has helped you to become a stone thrower and you believe you are a good stone thrower. But those beliefs and your confidence are about to be tested in your first competition.

Let's catch up with events as they occur on the Day of The Competition.

CHAPTER 23

How confident people think

In the morning before the competition, you're going through different scenarios in your head.

You might be thinking "Well this should be fun, plodding down to the Battle of Mojacar Playa to face certain defeat at the hands of The Spanish Stone Throwing Armada who have been firing stones into the sea since the sixteenth century."

You need to be thinking:

1. *So what if I crash out in the first round? One defeat doesn't suddenly make me a bad stone thrower.*

2. *It won't feel too bad because ten others are likely to be knocked out with me.*

3. *The lessons learnt in defeat will make me a better performer.*

You start to feel better but this only lasts until you climb onto the raised platform. Your arrival on the platform is met with boos from the strongly partisan local crowd.

You might be thinking "Outrageous behaviour! What

could I possibly have done to deserve these boos?" You need to be thinking:

1. *Not everyone wants me to win.*

2. *It doesn't mean there is anything wrong with me or them.*

You check your surname and remember you are not Spanish. You understand that with such a strong Mojacan presence, any outsider is likely to be booed and sure enough you hear other foreign competitors getting the same treatment. Now it's time for a few practice throws before the competition starts, to help you loosen up and get going.

You might be thinking "How do I know if I'm any good or not? Just because I can hit the target in practice whilst sitting in a deckchair blindfolded using my left hand to post on Instagram, it doesn't mean I'm a good stone thrower".

You need to be thinking:

1. *I am a good stone thrower because I have followed The Process.*

2. *If I can throw well in practice then why shouldn't I throw well in the competition?*

You have a good practice session, hitting the ten metre target three times with ten throws. As a result you've stopped feeling quite so nervous. The competition starts and out of the corner of your eye you see one of the entrants, Maria Fabregas, throwing her first stone. It crashes into the centre of the target with a loud bang. Maria looks like a formidable woman with a physique that would intimidate a Russian Olympic shot-putter.

You might be thinking "Let the disaster unfold".
You need to be thinking:

1. *It's time to forget about her performance and focus on my own.*

2. *Anyway, the competition has only just started and that is one throw.*

3. *Everyone has a spell in a competition when they play well and when they don't. This might be her strong spell.*

You start to breathe slowly and deeply and straight away you feel calmer. This allows you to put Maria's first throw into perspective. You are able to move on.

CHAPTER 24

How confident people behave

The first round is now well underway and as you look across the strip you see stone throwers effortlessly smashing the target as you miss the target with your first five stones.

You might be thinking "This is going well...another five throws like that and it's over".

You need to be saying:

1. *I'm going to be brave even if I don't feel it.*

2. *So, instead of collapsing into a heap, giving up and going home, I'm going to carry on.*

You manage to get a grip of yourself and your nerves and you hit the target with your next stone. You go on to hit the target for the fifth time with two stones to spare. You feel a sense of relief wash over you and also a sense of achievement as you qualify for the second round.

In the second round you start brightly and hit the target with your first three stones... stands back in amazement! A quick check of the scoreboard sees you out in front... but something happens as you then start to miss throw after throw. You're now struggling to stay in the competition as each missed throw moves you nearer to the exit door. After 15 throws you have still only hit the target *three* times.

You might be thinking "If I don't qualify for the final after being so far ahead, then I'm going to get slaughtered in the Mojacar Times this week".

You need to be saying:

1. *I'm going to slow my game down.*

2. *I'm therefore going to take my time and steady myself before each throw.*

You manage to slow yourself down and with your second to last stone you hit the target for the fifth time. However, the umpire's gaze has been momentarily averted by two dodgy looking characters selling beer back to the spectators from whom they stole it. The umpire is adamant that the stone, which admittedly had hit the outer edge of the target, has not hit the target at all. You inform the umpire about the mistake that he's making. The umpire responds with a shrug and informs you that you're incorrect and his decision is final.

You might *now* be thinking, "The umpire is clearly wrong and I'm going to tell the umpire exactly what I think about his decision just before I shove him into the sea".

You need to be saying:

1. *Yes, the umpire is clearly wrong.*

2. *However I am going to accept his decision because I cannot change it.*

You allow yourself a little smile and something inside of you let's go of the point. It's your twentieth and final throw of the second round and you need to hit the target with this final throw to stay in the competition. Deep breathing and slowing the game down are definitely helping you now. The stone leaves your hand and sails high into the air, smashing the target in the middle circle, making an almighty crack of a noise.

Well done... you made it to the final. This is again best of 20 throws. It turns out that only *one* other competitor has made it to the final (don't ask what would have happened if no-one had qualified) and its, you've guessed it, Maria Fabregas. In the final you're taking alternate throws and Maria has won the toss to throw first.

Maria starts strongly and after five throws each, she's leading 3-0. Maria hits the target with throw six and you miss *again* to make it 4-0 down. You're seriously struggling to get going and on her seventh throw she misses the target by an inch whilst you miss it by considerably more, nearly making it 5-0 down. You finally lose patience with yourself and start to go ballistic, kicking your pile of stones and your water bottle into the sea.

You might now be thinking you've lost. There is no way back from 4-0 down... it's over.

You need to be saying:

1. *I'm in a tough situation here and need to be kind to myself.*

2. *If I make another mistake during the competition then I'm going to forgive myself.*

You put your towel over your head and you start to well up. It's okay because you realise that you're doing your best and whatever happens you still made it to the Final. Something inside of you relaxes and you start to throw properly again. You're really flying now. After ten throws you pull it back to 4-2 and after 15 throws your leading 6-4! You're so close now, you can almost taste the champagne at the back your throat. If you hit the target *once* more in the next five throws that should clinch it... but you start to tighten up.

After 18 throws each, your lead has been cut to 6-5. On the 19th throw Maria misses again. If you hit the target with this throw then you've won. You miss... shit! It's Maria's twentieth and final throw and she hits the target with a beautiful gliding lob to make it 6-6... but you still have a chance to win *if* you hit the target with your final throw.

You miss *again*. You feel crushed because you tell yourself you blew it. You and Maria will now go into a play-off where the winner is the competitor who hits the target the most times with five throws.

CHAPTER 25

How confident people talk to themselves

The play-off begins. Maria throws first. She hits the target on the inner circle with a sublime full toss. Your turn now. Your arm feels like jelly and as you let go of the stone you hold on for slightly too long and miss the target by almost *five* metres! The missed opportunity in the final is clearly still playing on your mind as Maria walks up to take her second throw and it scrapes the outer edge of the target; but it still counts.

You're now hearing clearly a voice inside your head. You'll have come across the voice inside your head. If it's working with you, then everything is fine but if it isn't then there's only going to be one ending, and it isn't a good one. The voice *you* are hearing is a Critical Voice.

This is the voice that has been planted in your head as a child. Many people, who've had critical parents (75% and you're celebrating!), siblings, relatives or whatever, find this harsh voice inside their heads, criticising their best efforts and rarely offering praise or encouragement.

Anyway, back to the game... the Critical Voice is

coming through loud and clear as you take your stance to make your second throw. You've almost given up now, with Maria 2-0 ahead in the play-off, and, sure enough, you proceed to miss your second throw to keep the score at 2-0 down with three throws to go. You've now missed the target a total of seven times on the trot and your game has gone to pieces.

In your head you hear:

Critical Voice – "You fecking loser... are you trying to chuck this match away?"

You – "No I'm not."

Critical Voice – "Really. Missing the target seven times on the trot... you need bloody shooting".

You – "Okay Critical Voice, you win. I am utterly useless and you are absolutely right."

You know that you're on the verge of losing the game but something inside you refuses to quit. You ask the umpire for a toilet break (not normally allowed during a play-off but you mention last night's curry) and the umpire allows it. You need to try and regroup.

You climb into the plastic portable toilet and instead of continuing the conversation with the Critical Voice inside your head, you take the conversation out of your head. From now on, you talk to yourself out loud. Even better, you look at yourself in the mirror, deep into your eyes, while you're talking to yourself. You're now drilling into your mind the thoughts and beliefs you want to have. Stuff that will support you. You're now hearing yourself say the words:

1. *I've done well to get to the final.*

2. *If I've given it everything then I can accept losing.*

3. *If I focus on the performance then the result will take care of itself.*

This is proving to be a very powerful exercise because you can sense a gradual quietening of the old Critical Voice, replacing it with a new Nurturing Voice.

As you walk out of the toilet something strange has happened. You've accepted that you may lose. You no longer feel anxious. You start to relax and are now able to focus on your game.

Maria approaches the white line to take her third throw. If she hits the target and you miss, she wins. She misses. Yes! You're back in it. The next stone leaves your hand and it's a beautiful throw, hitting the target bang on the inner circle; the same spot where Maria's first throw landed. The score is 2-1 down with two to play. You're back in it. Maria throws next and misses again by half a metre. The pressure is getting to her and this spurs you on. You hit the target right on the outer edge, but this time the umpire saw it and, more importantly, it counts. The score stands at 2-2 with one throw left. Maria goes first and misses by the width of a fly's credit card. You know that if you hit the target you win. You step up and throw a lovely stone but it's a miss. It's a miss but you're okay. You're throwing well and that's what matters, as you and Maria go into the Sudden Death stage of the competition.

Sudden Death means that the first competitor to hit the target, when the other misses, wins the competition.

The Nurturing Voice tells you to relax and enjoy the competition... nothing else.

Maria throws first and hits the target. The pressure is on you to hit the target but you don't feel it because, even though you want to win, you don't *need* to any more. You save the match by making a solid throw and hit the middle circle of the target to make it 1-1. Maria takes her next throw and misses. It's your third chance to win the competition.

The Nurturing Voice tells you you're going to hit the target.

For a brief moment you visualise hitting the target on the near side of the inner circle. You throw the stone and it lands in the exact place. It's in. You win. You've won. Nice one!

Maria looks downcast as she shakes your hand and you realise it could have been you. You say a few kind words to her before you stand on the podium to receive the trophy. You did it. You can't help thinking to yourself how important it is to talk to yourself in the right way. It can be the difference between winning and losing.

CHAPTER 26

The role of the Nurturing Voice

In the last three chapters, we've worked out that by *thinking, behaving* and *talking to yourself* like a confident person then you will perform like a confident person. However, the one feature that sits behind these three actions, and is common to all of them, is the Nurturing Voice. What, you might ask, is the Nurturing Voice actually doing?

You'll notice that, during the competition, each time a fear came into your head you were able to overcome it:

1. When Maria smashed the target with her first throw, you were able to accept that everyone has good patches and bad patches during a game. She started well, that's all. (Fear of competing against a better player).

2. When the umpire made a mistake, you were able to accept that he had made a mistake and there was nothing you could do about it. (Fear that the umpire is biased).

3. When you were 4-0 down in the final and you put the towel over your head, had a little cry

and re-grouped, you were able to accept that you were playing badly and forgive yourself for doing so. (Fear of playing badly).

4. In the play-off where your Critical Voice came back to rear its ugly head you were able to accept that you might lose and you were okay with that as long as you had given it everything. (Fear of losing).

This was your Nurturing Voice operating at a very low volume in your head, trying to help you counter the fear by advising you in each situation. The message each time from your Nurturing Voice was essentially: *try and accept the situation as it stands.* Acceptance does not mean giving up, it means giving you back the energy you have lost through fear.

As a result, your energy was restored and you felt confident. The feeling of confidence allowed you to perform and you went on to win. This is because confidence is simply the energy you need to perform.

Confidence is performance energy.

CHAPTER 27

How to build the Nurturing Voice

As you can see from your magnificent win against Maria, if you start talking out loud to yourself in a positive way, sooner or later, the Critical Voice will be replaced with a new Nurturing Voice. What happens after a while is that you'll no longer need to speak out loud in order to help you perform well. The Nurturing Voice will have taken root in your head, ready to help you whenever you need it.

Your next question will therefore be, "How do I build this Nurturing Voice?" Well, quite simply, you need to *start* the habit of talking positively to yourself.

Let's start with where to build your Nurturing Voice. The place to build the Nurturing Voice is not in the middle of a competition when you're getting a good hiding. It's in a relaxed environment such as your own home, where you have the privacy to talk to yourself out loud. Obviously you don't really want people listening to you when you're talking to yourself as it generates all sorts of difficult to answer questions such as "Ever thought about finding yourself a real person to talk to... you know, like a friend?" but you can talk to yourself in the shower where no-one will hear you, or if you're driving, people won't think you're going mad, they'll simply think you're using the hands-free to explain to your managing director your behaviour at the conference in Blackpool last weekend. And all the time, you're building the habit of talking positively to yourself.

The place to build your Nurturing Voice is important because you need to talk to yourself out loud. This is an important detail in self-talk, because if you cannot *hear* the words you are saying, then those words floating around your head as thoughts have less impact. A great place to talk to yourself is in front of a mirror? Even better is to look deep into your eyes while you're doing it and put some real emotion into what you're saying. Well, what am I supposed to say to myself, I can hear your next question ringing in my ears? The simple answer to that is you must only say positive things to yourself:

When I want to motivate myself – I might use general banter like, "Hingo you're looking great today, I can see another Neil Deal coming out of that office this morning".

I might wish to compliment myself. "Neil, you did so well at swimming yesterday, I've never seen such fish-like qualities in you". Also call yourself by your own name. It seems to have more power when someone else is telling you how good you are.

A conversation about a problem might be the order of the day. I might start the conversation with asking myself a question... such as, "Hingo, you're looking a little bit stressed today, is there anything we need to sort out?" I'll then go on to have a little daddy talk with myself which ends up with me accepting that I'm not going on tour as resident drummer for the Tragic Street Porters.

All these sorts of statements and conversations help to build a kind Nurturing Voice which you need when you test your skills in a competitive environment.

When you've built yourself a new state-of-the-art Nurturing Voice you may wish to road test it in a competitive environment such as... your next stone throwing competition.

The thing to do then, is write down a few powerful sentences which are targeted to help you overcome your fears during the competition. Say them to yourself before you go into the competition and when you're competing. The golden rule is that these statements must be believable and personal to you, which is why I'm not going to write them for you. In fairness I *have* written everything else.

I have now left a little gap on the page for you to have a bash at writing out a few of them.

GAP ON PAGE

Don't try and be clever by trying to draft the perfect piece of prose, you're making a start here... you're not supposed to be an expert! Any old statements will do. It's only by using them, you'll work out if they're any good or not. If you're really struggling then I suppose you can use some of the statements (written in italics) that came into your head, when you beat Maria, to help you. Oh, and by the way, it would have been a good idea to go through this book with a pencil underlining the bits you felt meant most to you and making notes along the way. But thinking about it, I should really have mentioned that at the beginning of the book and not at the end of Chapter 27.

So, the moral of the story is... start talking to yourself... out loud. You will be amazed at how much better you'll perform, even if it means that people think you're going slightly maaaaaaddddd!!!

CHAPTER 28

Conclusion

M ost people think that you're born good at a skill or you're not, and if you're not, then there's nothing you can do about it. They also think that you're born confident at performing that skill or you're not, and if you're not then there's nothing you can do about that either. But I know different. The many challenges that I have overcome, have shown me, beyond reasonable doubt your honour, that you can train yourself to be good at a skill and confident at performing it.

To be good at a skill is very straightforward. You simply follow The Process which I have listed neatly in bullet points at the end of Chapter 21. So what was the point, you may ask, of the first 20 chapters above when all you really needed was a couple of lines detailing The Process? The point of all those chapters above is that they bring The Process to life, which is not possible with a single page of bullet points. I also believe that when you read about me blowing 175,000 euros on a deal you won't feel quite as bad about your own mistakes.

To be truly confident at performing a skill, you need to change the voice inside your head to a Nurturing Voice. This voice will help you eliminate fear by accepting the situation. This will lead to you becoming a more confident performer. The Nurturing Voice will grow in your head if you're willing to invest just a few minutes a day on building it.

The link between The Process and confidence is that when you've been through The Process, you will feel confident. However, this confidence might not last long during a performance without the assistance of the Nurturing Voice. You need the help of the Nurturing Voice to defend you against fear, otherwise you may run out of performance energy.

The main focus of this book has been The Process because I wanted you to get the message that it's the *learning* from your mistakes that is the gold. The problem is that most people get disheartened when failure comes around, which it naturally has to, in order for you to succeed. They attach all sorts of superstition and negative beliefs to the failure, like "Well I'm unlucky, so I was bound to fail". They ignore the fact that they haven't practised for six months or they revised for one topic in an exam where five were being tested.

If you can take the learning from each mistake without giving up then you really cannot avoid improving... no matter how hard you try to screw up!

Oh, you might be wondering whatever happened to good old Noddy White. Well, despite all my pleading, Noddy refused point blank to help me with the writing of this book. Not out of malice I hasten to add... modesty. You see, Noddy didn't think he was special being good at anything, he thought anybody could do it. Maybe now you believe him.

THE END

Acknowledgements

I would just like to acknowledge my debt of gratitude to West Midlands Railway and thank them for providing me with office accommodation and somewhere to sleep while I wrote this book. The fact that they took me to work and back each day was a particularly nice touch.

I would like to thank my wife Sophie for marrying me (best decision ever... mine not hers) and for her patience... because my goodness she needs it.

I would like to thank Baby Nancy for helping me answer her questions more quickly by kicking the back of my seat with both feet when I'm driving.

I would like to thank Charlie, my son, for road testing the stories in this book. His contribution was made all the more surprising when you consider that Charlie went from the Argos catalogue Lego section to the Next catalogue lingerie section and managed to miss out literature all together.

My thanks must also go to the following people who were subjected to the third draft and were extremely kind about the book's prospects of survival even when it was clear that it required major surgery:

Alexandra Seymour   *Johnny Lake*
Sarah Platts   *Sarah Veasey*
Matt Baker   *Kirsten Bolton*
Josh Richardson   *Caitlin Quilty*
Mark Richardson   *Stef Davies*
Sally Abrol
Kel Richardson (I got a discount for using
three Richardsons)

Thanks also to the additional people who came on board to read the far less painful sixth version:

Andrew Bradley   *Louise Young*
Matt Page   *Lucy Fincher-Giles*
June Hall   *Damien Kearns*
Renée Tombs   *Seb Isaacs*
Helen Bradshaw   *Natalie Ashby*

I would like to thank Griff and Gary for doing our garden. The whole book-writing adventure was made so much easier knowing that our garden was in safe hands during these challenging times.

I would like to thank Richard Troll for having such a great surname and being the last person to leave Sophie's 50th... by 45 minutes!!!

Richard Ash, Anna Targett, Sally Gilbert, Sophie Targett and Helen Bradshaw – For providing guidance on front cover.

Cameron Holland – For providing front cover.

Mum and Dad... where do I start?

Aunty June – *You* are the Alchemist.

Jag – For operating the best offy in the country at Willow Court Wines with a not too shabby 452 brands of gin on sale.

Lee – For services to Illegal Printing.

Lucy Frontani – For putting it all together and always being on my side.

And finally, I would like to thank Andy *Sharewatch* Bradshaw for cutting his rain-soaked lawn using a battery-operated mower with the power of an electric toothbrush. No finer display of man versus machine am I ever likely to witness.

When I was young, I used to watch my dad in action and I noticed that whenever something went wrong, sooner or later he would laugh about it. He never told me why he did this and it was only after he died that I thought about it and worked it out. The reason he laughed was because laughing is the best way to get over something. The best bit is that when you're over it, you can learn from it. Try this today when something goes wrong.

Printed in Great Britain
by Amazon

80642155R00081